What people are saying about this book?

When I think of prayer warriors, I think of Carol Gordon. When I consider whom to call when a couple is waging war and doing spiritual battle in defense of their marriage, I think of Carol Gordon.

Carol is a woman of faith who has learned that truth prevails, victory is ours for the taking, and healing is available for everyone through Jesus. Through Carol's own life and her struggles in her own marriage, she found that place of sweet release through the power of repentance, forgiveness, and healing. A writer's words are most powerful when truth has been born out of adversity and triumph! One would do well to spend time meditating on the words of this anointed author and friend of all!

Mike Jestes
Oklahoma Chairman of the National Day of Prayer

In *Connections*, Carol Gordon has offered a "how to hug" manual to the body of Christ. Carol is a practitioner—she lives out these principles in her daily walk with Jesus and in expressing her love to others. You will be enriched and equipped to strengthen the lives of others as you read and put into practice the powerful insights taught in this book.

John Youell
Pastor, The Crown Center OKC
Director, Oklahoma City Metro Prayer Alliance

Carol Gordon believes all of life plays out in how we do relationships and how we connect with others. In her new book *Connections*, Carol shares fresh insight into important biblical principles and truths concerning relationships in our marriages and families. I am happy to recommend *Connections*.

Marilyn Conrad
Founder and President (retired), Covenant Keepers, Inc.

In *Connections*, Carol Gordon details healthy ways to form and maintain relationships based on scriptural guidance. Carol's book is an excellent resource on how to reference God's Word for lasting and vibrant human connections. This book demonstrates the key components for nourishing and fruitful human bonds in all areas of life.

Kristy Rogers
Bachelor of Science from Rogers State University
Master of Human Relations from Oklahoma University

Every time Carol Gordon has begun working on a new teaching or book, I have seen how much of its content comes out of her life. She has been a living example to many.

The way God forms, assembles, and causes the body of Christ to function only becomes visible as we pray and come into one accord through divine connections. This subject has been a lifelong journey that Carol has searched out and lived.

All of us who read this book should embrace both the simple and the sweeping changes in our relationships, because letting our Creator jointly fit us with others is His great design and the pattern found in Scripture. A divinely connected body is one full of His presence and glory.

I would encourage you to read *Connections* and reread it as many times as necessary until you can pray for God to order your steps and rearrange everything in your life according to His ways and designs. Then hold onto covenant with Jesus and those He connects you with.

Timothy Bence
President, Covenant Connections

Connections is certainly a great work that evidences Carol Gordon's insight from having served many years of ministry and counseling. Carol skillfully uses the principles and guidelines of God's plan from Scripture that dynamically and sometimes uniquely apply to relationships, especially marriage. I believe the instructions within this book will help and strengthen any relationship. Here you will find answers that you will wish you had discovered long ago.

Jerry Maston
Pastor, River of Life Church; Eastland, Texas
President, Leadership Always
Founder, Christian Values Summit

Carol Gordon does a masterful job Scripturally highlighting the way God created us for connection, the hindrances to connection, and the tools to maintain solid, loving, trusting connection with God, man, and even ourselves. If you ever wondered why you or someone you love seems unconnected, or perhaps keeps connecting to the wrong things, Carol shares her personal experience and wisdom into the deep forces that impact our connections. The reality is, we are all relational beings, and life is filled with relationship connections. This book will give you practical insights to make sure your relationships are God-honoring, love-reflecting, comfort-receiving, and communicated in a way that builds up everyone. The end result is a healthy heart where the comfort of the Holy Spirit allows us to connect fearlessly with a God who loves us unconditionally, and empowers us to maximize the divine-connections He has set before us.

Pastor Robert Altemus
Pastor of Faith Community Fellowship in Universal City
Texas

CONNECTIONS

BY CAROL GORDON

Foreword
BY CLARENCE HILL

Connections

Copyright © 2016

H M Publishing Company
PO Box 141
Eastland, TX 76448-0141

Cover design by Eryn J Carlisle

Printed in the United States of America
ISBN 978-0-9906124-9-0

Dedication

That their hearts may be encouraged, being knit together in love, and attaining to all riches of the full assurance of understanding, to the knowledge of the mystery of God, both of the Father and of Christ, in whom are hidden all the treasures of wisdom and knowledge.
—Colossians 2:2–3

With great love, I dedicate this book to my children, Steven Ridgeway, Katherine Louise, and Jennifer Elizabeth, treasures of my heart. I am thankful for their forgiveness of my failures and for their love and encouragement. We were the Father's choice for this family "knitting," and I am blessed by what I have learned from them and Him.

I thank them and their spouses for my grandchildren, who are likewise treasures.

I am also thankful for the many "spiritual children" the Lord has blessed me with along the way!

I know the Lord has great plans and purposes for all of them!

Table Of Contents

Foreword

I live in Oklahoma City, part of the infamous "tornado alley." In this part of the country, it is common to hear chilling stories of why families finally paid the price to purchase a storm shelter. I've heard of close calls, where the tornado's path seemed to be planning a direct hit on a family's home, and I have also heard stories where neighbors lost almost everything. In some way, a situation hit close enough to home to make the threat a reality.

I couldn't think of a better analogy to explain this book. Relationships are suffering, and this book is the storm shelter. People are hurt, fearful, and overly cautious. Some of our lives and destinies have actually been thrown off course by failed relationships with spouses, parents, children, and friends. It seems that "tornado alley" has become more than just Oklahoma and Kansas when it comes to relationships.

I have been amazed at the practicality Mrs. Carol has provided in *Connections*. The truths and principles in this book are the three-foot thick walls of safety that could only come from someone who has lived them out.

I will never forget when I first met Mrs. Carol over ten years ago. I remember how it was the warmth of her welcome, which gave me an unexpected level of comfort and confidence to sit at a table of strangers and share my fledgling vision for healing marriages and families. She wasn't even leading the meeting, but she broke protocol to patiently express her joy in me. I'm having trouble trying to explain what happened, but her genuine joy and celebration over my little efforts gave me confidence and a real assurance that God was with me.

Since that day I have loved Mrs. Carol and watched her live out what she has written in this book. I am challenged to know that I can one day be so forgiving, gracious, and genuine. There are no excuses now! Mrs. Carol has been led to write these truths for us and our children in this book.

If you ever have the chance to meet her, you will understand why I celebrate her. Her trust in God is pure, and her wisdom is proven. I never experienced a holy hug from her and her husband, but one of the couples they mentored has become like a personal marriage coach to my wife and me.

Before I read this book, I knew Mrs. Carol had great depth, but I had no idea she would provide this much biblical substance in such a practical way. I am honored to have been invited to write the foreword for this spiritual storm shelter called *Connections*. Enjoy and put to practice what you read.

Clarence Hill, Jr.
Pastor, Church Ablaze
Founder, Eye to Eye Marriage Community
Oklahoma City, OK

The Key of Connecting

All of life plays out in how we do relationships. Our heavenly Father designed us to be connected to one another. Father's first relationship structure was a married couple, and from there He planned families to continue in joyful, healthy connection forever. We can see this pattern in the way He detailed family genealogy in the Old Testament.

Have you ever been encouraged by someone's testimony of a healed relationship? Are you excited when a relationship works out for you? How do you feel when you reach an understanding with someone and suddenly know the person's heart? Perhaps you have been in pain because of something someone said, and you discover you totally misunderstood that person and his or her intent.

We've all experienced difficulties connecting with others. Because of past hurts and present misunderstandings, many of us throw away relationships that Father designed to be a blessing to us. Walking in fear that these relationships will continue to hurt (rather than working to resolve them), robs us of so much!

I received the following prophetic word in September 2007:

I hear the Lord saying that He has created Heart Menders with a unique fabric woven of many different kinds of threads—threads with different colors and textures. But the fabric that He has produced, while hard to understand by men, is beautiful to Him.

The DNA of Heart Menders is unique in the kingdom and cannot be compared with others. It is a DNA that was birthed out of many hours of prayer and intercession, travail, and spiritual warfare. And it is pleasing in the sight of the Lord. And the DNA of Heart Menders contains many different facets. It is not one thing or another. It is many things at once. When people see the various projects and outreaches and conferences and classes, they will say that Heart Menders is divided or lacks focus. "But it is all one," says the Lord. It is a richness of *tapestry* that I have created for my own purposes. It is interwoven by the Master Weaver with many different threads, but they all make up one *tapestry*. It is a reflection of Me," says the Lord.

Author Deborah Raney says that when we look at the part of our tapestry we can see, which is the back of the work, all we recognize are knots and loose threads. In reality these are connections in progress. Only in eternity does the Lord reveal the lovely, finished picture on the front of the tapestry.[1]

The ridiculous notion that we can live without connections is a huge deception from the enemy. God did not design us to be disconnected. This is the reason for the popularity of "social media." It gives the illusion of connection without requiring intimacy.

We are always connected to a "higher power." Hopefully, all of us choose the way of wholeness by receiving the Lord Jesus as our Savior. Our only default choice is Satan. We are always connected to one or the other—we are never independent. Thanks to Jesus, we do get to choose whom we serve!

Our enemy constantly works to use connections for evil. Strife, division, destruction, divorce, and many other traumas cause heartache and brokenness. The current exposure of the prevalence of bullying, abuse, pornography, and domestic violence indicates how much has been going on behind the scenes. Every hurt in life comes from broken and traumatic relationships.

The Lord said to my friend Terry Brim, a chemist, "Molecular compounds are the building blocks of My Hand!" We can see how true this concept is in the physical realm. Similarly, it is true in the spiritual realm: relational connections are the building blocks of our lives. We can't "do family" well, or at all, without first mending our hearts and learning to use the tools available for healing.

My late husband, Louis, and I experienced great healing and restoration in our relationship when we came to the Lord in the early 1980s. After limping through twenty-three years of marriage and hitting a wall, we knew little to nothing about having a healthy relationship. However, the Lord brought miraculous changes to our hearts and perceptions, and we made great progress in the upward direction under His tutelage. Even more amazing, He allowed us to partner with Him as He healed other hearts and marriages through us. As we gave "Father's blessings" and "Mommy and Daddy hugs" and repented for generational sins, the healing continued flowing to many others.

As we acknowledge past hurts—whether ours or our antecedents'—God can transform our relationships. In his book *Dominion*, Randy Alcorn, one of my favorite authors, gives a wonderful portrayal of the main character, Jake, repenting to his new friend, Clarence, for his forefathers' sins against Clarence's ancestors during the slavery era.[2] Jesus' blood paid for all sin. We are connected to our ancestors' sins, beginning as far back as Adam or Noah. Sin is a connector to death, just like the blood and glory are connectors to life. This is why "identificational repentance" works in restoring relationships, both individually and corporately. This is why the "Mommy and Daddy hugs" Louis and I gave worked. Setting things in right order in the Spirit realm is life giving.

The Hebraic word for *sacrifice* is *korban,* which means "drawing near."[3] When we bring a gift to the Lord—a sacrifice—it brings us close to Father and reconnects us to Him. His receiving of our gift, our sacrifice, connects us with His gift. Just as prayer connects us with Him, in a similar way it connects us with family, friends, teachers, and other precious ones.

For this reason, it is vital to understand the dynamics of connecting in a healthy way. Let's look more closely at how these dynamics work.

Connecting to the Lord

All through the Bible we see Father's design to bless us, His creation. He made a lovely place and then brought His children into it. When He created His first couple, He revealed more of His heart than we realize: *Then the rib which the Lord God had taken from man He made into a woman, and He brought her to the man. And Adam said: "This is now bone of my bones and flesh of my flesh; she shall be called Woman, because she was taken out of Man." Therefore a man shall leave his father and mother and be joined to his wife, and they shall become one flesh* (Gen. 2:22–24). Father's express purpose was for companionship and connection, solely to bless us.

Obviously the enemy came quickly to divide and separate. The history of mankind, apart from God, has been one of discord and endless strife.

Father endeavored to reconnect with man through covenant, which worked to bring back opportunities to bless. Yet too many times, man turned away from God to his own efforts.

Then Jesus came and showed us what it looked like to walk and talk like Father. His purpose was three-fold: to show us the Father's heart, to pay the ultimate sacrifice for our sin, and to provide the means for a permanent reconnect! Now we have been given connection with the source of grace and forgiveness!

Jesus used many illustrations to help us see heavenly realities. One favorite illustration is His comparison of our relationship with Him and the Father to familiar agricultural practices, found in John 15:1–8:

"I am the true vine, and my Father is the gardener. He cuts off every branch in me that bears no fruit, while every branch that does bear fruit he prunes so that it will be even more fruitful. You are already clean because of the word I have spoken to you. Remain in me, and I will remain in you. No branch can bear fruit by itself; it must remain in the vine. Neither can you bear fruit unless you remain in me.

"I am the vine; you are the branches. If a man remains in me and I in him, he will bear much fruit; apart from me you can do nothing. If anyone does not remain in me, he is like a branch that is thrown away and withers; such branches are picked up, thrown into the fire and burned. If you remain in me and my words remain in you, ask whatever you wish, and it will be given you. This is to my Father's glory, that you bear much fruit, showing yourselves to be my disciples" (NIV).

Through His death, burial, and resurrection, Jesus made this reconnection with our heavenly family possible. Romans 6:4–5 says, *Therefore we were buried with Him through baptism into death, that just as Christ was raised from the dead by the glory of the Father, even so we also should walk in newness of life. For if we have been united together in the likeness of His death, certainly we also shall be in the likeness of His resurrection.*

Without Jesus, even the best attempts of the Hebrew children to obey the Word were futile, leaving them, and us, still separated. Father gave the glory, the substance of heaven, to Jesus to glue us to Himself (see John 17: 22). By His grace and mercy, He made it possible for us to belong to Him again. His glory glues us together.

So many in the body of Christ do not really grasp that He came to live *in* us as the Holy Spirit—at Pentecost initially, and always as we receive Jesus as our Savior and Lord. This indwelling is the guarantee of our connectedness! We should rely on this presence with and in us at all times. He promised to be with us always—and Holy Spirit's indwelling is how He fulfills that promise. His presence in us is the most important connection that proceeds from our relationship with the Lord.

If this is a concept you have not yet made your own, do study through the New Testament letters and see how often they speak of being "in Him," "in Christ," and so on. Understanding this truth is life changing! We are never alone. He lives in us, and we live in Him!

The Scriptures also frequently use marriage to illustrate our unity with one another. *Therefore, my brethren, you also have become dead to the law through the body of Christ, that you may be married to another—to Him who was raised from the dead, that we should bear fruit to God* (Rom. 7:4). Ephesians 5 presents a challenge to us all through its vivid description of marriage as a picture of Christ and the church. (For an extended study of this subject, see my book *Marriage Is a Gift.*)

With marriage as an example, God's plan is an abundant life, with all aspects of this fundamental relationship growing and glowing. His goal is to see His character, nature, and glory reproduced in us! If we are experiencing any degree of that abundance, it will cause people to ask, "Wonder how they got that?"

The Lord is big on healthy connections! So how do we develop them?

- We adapt our lives to the directions He gives in His Word, while allowing His internal work to change our hearts.
- We sow into others' lives and then reap in own lives.
- We help somebody else even if we are only one step ahead of that person.
- We stay rooted in the Vine.
- We keep planting seed, knowing our Father is the Husbandman who causes the seed to grow.
- We catch the vision of sharing what God has given us, because this is how the kingdom has always grown.
- We pray over people we are in contact with.
- We act on what we know, and expect to see Him working.

Ephesians 4:13–16 clearly describes the goal:

'Til we all come to the unity of the faith and of the knowledge of the Son of God, to a perfect man, to the measure of the stature of the fullness of Christ; that we should no longer be children, tossed to and fro and car-ried about with every wind of doctrine, by the trickery of men, in the cunning craftiness of deceitful plotting, but, speaking the truth in love, may grow up in all things into Him who is the head—Christ—from whom the whole body, joined and knit together by what every joint supplies, according to the effective working by which every part does its share, causes growth of the body for the edifying of itself in love.

Speaking truth in love connects us with one another in a healthy way.

Mommy and Daddy hugs connected people with Jesus in an amazing way. Many have waited all their lives to hear someone who understood or inflicted their pain to say, "I re-pent." Jesus does understand our pain and joins in those hugs as He said He would. Healing words spoken in love literally change connections in the physical, emotional, and mental realms.

Speaking the truth in love is another vital component of effective connection. One of Jesus' favorite sayings was *"I tell you the truth"* (*"Verily, verily, I tell you the truth,"* in the King James Version). This *"I tell you the truth"* statement appears in Matthew thirty times; Mark, fifteen times; Luke, nine times; and John, twenty-five times. In addition, Jesus referred to Himself as truth (see John 14:6) and the Holy Spirit as truth (see John 14:17), and He told Pilate He came to bring truth (see John 18:37). Jesus also said in John 8:31–32 that "staying with" His words, His truth, sets us free. Furthermore, the apostle John said that Jesus was *"full of grace and truth"* (John 1:14).

The Ephesians 6:14 description of God's armor characterizes *truth* as "a belt around the loins." Scripture frequently uses the term *loins* to refer to "family." We protect our family by speaking truth in love. All truth originates in our Father, not in our opinions. We must speak truth to, with, and about one another.

Psalm 51:6 says, *Behold, You desire truth in the inward parts, and in the hidden part You will make me to know wisdom.* Since He desires truth, are we honest with ourselves? Do we have secrets we do not want exposed? Dishonesty will cause connections to be broken in disastrous ways.

We can maintain healthy connections in several ways. Prayer for ourselves and others is one. Early on, I prayed 1

Corinthians 1:27–30 to encourage myself that my husband could have wisdom. Over the years, the Lord noted other Scripture to pray for him. These prayers transformed my image of him and set him free to become the man of God he was called to be.

Past connections influence us. Men can still hear their mother's voice, and resist their wife's requests. Anytime we harbor offense, it will interfere with clear communication.

Father is clear: *[The purpose is] that through the church the complicated, many-sided wisdom of God in all its infinite variety and innumerable aspects might now be made known to the angelic rulers and authorities (principalities and powers) in the heavenly sphere* (Eph. 3:10 AMPC). Our view of life is linear: we see things in a natural order of events. The Lord's view is eternal and intricate. It looks one way to us here but will look entirely different when we see it from the perspective of eternity. I was going back over the prophetic word mentioned in the first chapter, and I was very encouraged. The Lord began to let me "see" a crosscut of the thick tapestry as a reminder. It is all about the intricate divine connections He is weaving. Some of the connections He has set up, we have undervalued. Others we have misunderstood, and allowed disappointment to blind us.

In the Lord, we can adopt an eternal mindset here and now. Early in Louis's and my marital healing process, I asked the Lord how He saw Louis. Gaining the Lord's perspective changed the way I viewed and related to Louis. We all need this same change of view when we're struggling in our relationships. Once we begin to see others through Father's eyes, we are more able to respond to these people with His love.

The Lord sets up connections His children will need in the future. One such connection was that of Joseph and Pharaoh's cupbearer, established while Joseph was a prisoner in Egypt. Several years before it was time for Joseph to step into leadership, God had Joseph minister to this cupbearer, the very person who would be on the spot when the time came for Joseph's dream to come to pass. The Lord works His plans out way ahead of time.

I had a wonderful experience along these lines. I sold some properties over a period years, and there was a mix-up in the paperwork by one of the financial agencies involved. After this problem came to light, it took almost another year to close on the final sale. Although I was praying and my lawyer was advising, the process was very slow.

At one point the Lord began to give me specific directions on the final step of dealing with the bank who owed me a refund. It took several weeks to finalize a meeting with the person who could make the decision. In the meantime I received a word from the Lord about some ministry He wanted me to conduct at a conference I was soon to attend.

I carried out this ministry for most of the people involved who attended the conference; however, there were some I did not see there. So a friend and I agreed to divide up the remaining individuals on the list: she would minister to part, and I would contact the rest. There was one very special person neither of us knew how to reach. We asked the Lord to help us find this person.

I came home from the conference and the next day went to the bank meeting. As it turned out, one of the men in the meeting was the grandson of the very woman I needed to find! I was so excited about locating her that the bank issue diminished in importance—although, in the end, I did receive a good portion of what was owed!

The Lord is always working with us and with others. We may see this work as struggles and trials, but He sees it as training, building, and causing growth! As such, we can compare life to a training facility, and marriage to one of the intense courses we must pass.

As I said before, all of life plays out in our relationships. Most people think life, and marriage in particular, is about their being happy. In case you haven't figured it out yet, that's not its purpose! The purpose of marriage is to manifest the love of the Lord. Have you noticed the toughest place to practice the love walk is often with the people you claim to love the most?

*For we are God's fellow workers; you are God's field, you are **God's building**. . . . But let each one take heed how he builds on it. . . . each one's work will become clear; for the Day will declare it, because it will be revealed by fire; and the fire will test each one's work, of what sort it is* (1 Cor. 3:9–13).

We build our lives, and if they are built in Him, they can stand the test when fiery trials come. Without Him we cannot build lasting, healthy relationships. *You also, as living stones, are **being built up** a spiritual house, a*

*holy priesthood, to offer up spiritual sacrifices accepta-
ble to God through Jesus Christ. Therefore it is also con-
tained in the Scripture, "Behold, I lay in Zion a chief
cornerstone, elect, precious, and he who believes on Him
will by no means be put to shame"* (1 Pet. 2:5–6).

The Holy Spirit is a strategic agent of change. Scripture
refers to Him as oil, fire, and water, and describes us as ves-
sels (see 2 Tim. 2:20). The cleansing process we go through
as we grow and change might be depicted as follows: Our
little vessel has some "gunk" in it. The Holy Spirit oil comes
in and softens the gunk. Then water fills the vessel and fire
ignites under the vessel to heat the water. The gunk rises and
is washed away. After a while, the whole process starts
again. (Does this progression sound familiar?)

Soon we learn to welcome His cleansing processes, because we have learned we will be refined in the midst of it.
His love prevents Him from leaving us like we were when
He began His work in us. Philippians 1:6 promises that He
will complete it.

Our Father shows His love for us by pouring out more
grace each time we need it. We respond with the "Yes!" of
faith to this magnificent gift of grace. *But without faith it is*

impossible to please Him, for he who comes to God must be-
lieve that He is, and that He is a rewarder of those who dil-
igently seek Him (Heb. 11:6). The closer we grow to Him
through prayer and worship, the more we trust Him to heal
our broken relationships. We find ourselves resting in *joy*
even when the circumstances do not look promising.

Therefore, *trust in the LORD with all your heart, and*
lean not on your own understanding; in all your ways
acknowledge Him, and He shall direct your paths (Prov.
3:5–6). As you trust and rely on Him, He will make you more
like Himself—able to build and rebuild healthy connections.
Trust that His hand is working in every circumstance, weaving His purpose for you and through you *even when you*
can't see it yet—for yourself and especially for your loved
ones. As 2 Corinthians 4:18 says, *Do not look at the things*
which are seen, but at the things which are not seen. For the
things which are seen are temporary, but the things which
are not seen are eternal.

Comfort is a major way we *receive* connection. If we are
not comfortable and don't feel safe with another person, we
will not connect with that person in a healthy way. In the

busyness of our days, we have interactions with many people, both in and away from the home, and we experience more disappointed expectations than we realize or admit. We usually tough it out and go on our way.

Second Corinthians 1:3–4 gives us instructions: *Blessed be the God and Father of our Lord Jesus Christ, the Father of mercies and God of all comfort, who comforts us in all our tribulation, that we may be able to comfort those who are in any trouble, with the comfort with which we ourselves are comforted by God.* Are we admitting our need for comfort? Are we receiving the Lord's consistent love and comfort for us?

Are we comforting our spouse? Are we taking responsibility for our part in disappointing our spouse? Are we being a comfort to our children? Parents disappoint children all the time and are totally unaware of it. Most people need more comforting than they acknowledge. Let's be alert to comfort and nurture our loved ones. It is important to our Father.

Second Corinthians 5:17–21 teaches us that when we are safe, with God or our spouse, there is amazing reconciliation. As long as we are unsure that we are loved, the walls remain. Relationship is birthed and grown where there is comfort—

when we are at ease with another: having no fear, being received by that person, and feeling safe. When we are comfortable, we can safely respond, trust, and expect good things.

The comfort we receive as infants determines our connection to our parents. We receive where we are comfortable. Our enemy makes early preemptive strikes to divide us from our parents. If we don't feel safe, we won't relax and open ourselves to heart relationships, and we will be vulnerable to injury. When there is fear in an early relationship, we shut down in some areas and become twisted in others. The parental relationship is primary in determining whether we are whole, healthy, and joy-filled.

So I returned, and considered all the oppressions that are done under the sun: and behold the tears of such as were oppressed, and they had no comforter; and on the side of their oppressors there was power; but they had no comforter (Eccl. 4:1 KJV). There is no comfort for the oppressed or for their oppressors. Both operate in fear and shame.

Have you seen any TV shows like that? Our culture is now making "entertainment" out of exposing wounds and trauma. The enemy works to keep us wounded and produce more trauma. He wants us to remember and relive old hurts.

One example of such damage is teen girls who "conform" to whatever the current boyfriend expects until they lose their identity. They believe they must be what others expect—whether on an individual or corporate level. They have not developed identity because they have not experienced safe connection, comfort, or affirmation. Real security lies in knowing who they are in Christ and resting in that knowledge. The kind of "fathering" they receive is crucial.

The enemy will keep harassing us until we no longer *know* what we have and who we are *in Christ*. His modus operandi is to bring fear, shame, and separation, which produce an "orphan spirit." An orphan feels he is alone and must fend for, provide for, and protect himself. Jesus said, "[No way!] *I will not leave you orphans; I will come to you* " (John 14:18).

The Holy Spirit is the Comforter. He connects us in the Trinity. Jesus came so that we could connect with Him without fear. Many have been taught to fear Father's character and, as such, don't recognize Him in the Son. Remember, Jesus said that He came to show us the Father.

We can trust Father with our safety. Father gives continued assurance of His mercy and grace. It is *always* His character to comfort. Isaiah 51:12, 13, and 15 says,

"I, even I, am He who comforts you. Who are you that you should be afraid of a man who will die, and of the son of a man who will be made like grass? And you forget the LORD your Maker, who stretched out the heavens and laid the foundations of the earth; you have feared continually every day because of the fury of the oppressor, when he has prepared to destroy. And where is the fury of the oppressor? But I am the LORD your God, who divided the sea whose waves roared—the LORD of hosts is His name."

In John 14:16–17, Jesus said, *"And I will ask the Father, and He will give you another Comforter (Counselor, Helper, Intercessor, Advocate, Strengthener, and Standby), that He may remain with you forever—the Spirit of Truth, whom the world cannot receive (welcome, take to its heart), because it does not see Him or know and recognize Him. But you know and recognize Him, for He lives with you [constantly] and will be in you"* (AMPC).

Jesus also said, *"Nevertheless I tell you the truth; it is expedient for you that I go away: for if I go not away, the Comforter will not come unto you; but if I depart, I will send him unto you"* (John 16:7 KJV; see also John 16:13–14; Hebrews 13:5–6). When we allow the Lord to be our comfort, we can connect with others in a healthy way. His comfort brings healing in our other relationships. When we draw from His reservoir of comfort to give to others, it eases our way of connecting with and comforting them. Reconciliation is our assignment. Reread 2 Corinthians 5:17–21, using *"comfort"* in place of *"reconcile."*

Holy Spirit always keeps us connected to Jesus in a loving, trusting relationship. *"But when the Comforter is come, whom I will send unto you from the Father, even the Spirit of truth, which proceedeth from the Father, he shall testify of me"* (John 15:26 KJV). We may appear to be alone, but we are never so! Many other scriptures bear this out.

In John 14:26, we read, *"But the Comforter, which is the Holy Ghost, whom the Father will send in My name, He shall teach you all things, and bring all things to your remembrance, whatsoever I have said unto you"* (KJV). The Comforter will work His healing *grace* to set us free. When we cooperate, He renews our mind, revealing our true identity. Learning that we are safe in Him is vital. We can build an "I am safe" net with Psalms 23 and 91.

Blessed be God, even the Father of our Lord Jesus Christ, the Father of mercies, and the God of all comfort; who comforteth us in all our tribulation, that we may be able to comfort them which are in any trouble, by the comfort wherewith we ourselves are comforted of God (2 Cor. 1:3–4 KJV).

We have many opportunities to honor the Lord and each other through godly connections. In marriage, we can honor one another by receiving new views of our spouse from the Lord, by praying to the One who hears, and by using kind words. God gives us all we need, plus the handbook for knowing His ways: *Beloved, I pray that you may prosper in all things and be in health, just as your soul prospers"* (3 John 2).

The Divider

It is clear that God's opponent plots and plans to sever us from the source of our identity, purpose, and power. God's enemy corrupts and misdirects the purpose of connection through unhealthy connections, negative or absence of touch, sexual sin, or various other types of abuse. Such abuse causes misfires in our soul that blind us and disconnect us from Father's purpose.

In biblical history we see that two of Noah's sons distanced themselves from God's specific direction to spread out over the earth. Instead, they tried to stay banded together to meet their own needs without God. Their disobedience led to competition, wars, and eventually the total loss of the strength of communication, unity, and agreement.

The church did just the opposite of what the Lord instructed as well. At first, believers stayed close to home and had no vision to cover the earth. When they did move out, they had great fruit, but then the newcomers divided from their Jewish roots. One church existed for a thousand years. Then the church split into two branches—eastern and western. After another five hundred years, the church divided further. From there, divisions over doctrine escalated to the point that, now, the church now has over thirty-three thousand different groups! This disunity plays right into the enemy's hands. All he has to do is get someone offended, puffed up in pride or nursing hurt feelings, and the person sets love aside.

In Ephesians 4:17–19, Paul says, *This I say, therefore, and testify in the Lord, that you should no longer walk as the rest of the Gentiles walk, in the futility of their mind, having their understanding darkened, being alienated from the life of God, because of the ignorance that is in them, because of the blindness of their heart.* We are no longer to live as the world does.

Even in good families, it may be normal for us to harden our hearts when we are hurt or disappointed. The battle with our flesh is constant. Dr. Bill Gillham, in his book *Lifetime Guarantee*, notes that even if we are successful in life, without the Lord, our success is "USDA choice flesh!"[1]

Hurting people hurt other people. Children who are not "heard" or honored will disconnect in bitterness. How many lives could we change and hearts soften by laying aside our selfishness and listening with our hearts to one another?

Learning and applying new communication skills is a challenge that bears great fruit. Saying with sincerity "I want to hear how you see this" and listening without self-defense bring healing.

The prophet Isaiah said, *"Cry aloud, spare not; lift up your voice like a trumpet; tell My people their transgression, and the house of Jacob their sins"* (Isa. 58:1). We must see the truth of how the enemy divides us. We must shout aloud the disobedience of our hard hearts. We must refuse to justify ourselves (our sin) out of hardness of heart, which disconnects and separates.

After my precious husband and I had spent many hours praying for our older daughter, we began to see a work of redemption in her life. Later, when struggles were ongoing between Louis and both our daughters, I fasted and prayed. I stood on Proverbs 20:27, *"The spirit of man is the candle of the LORD, searching all the inward parts of the belly"* (KJV). I also prayed Mark 4:22, *"There is nothing hidden that shall not be revealed."*

The Lord spoke to Louis, revealing an area that was keeping him bound up and causing hurt to his children. He repented and healing began.

We have since used Mark 4:22 many times as we bring someone before the Lord and ask Him to reveal to that person his/her own heart. No matter how close we are to an individual, only the Lord knows the person's heart. We connect with the Holy Spirit, rib-to-rib, as we pray in the Spirit for the person. Then we trust the Lord to reveal what needs to be seen.

How parents deal with their children has a far-reaching effect. The Word puts great emphasis on the importance of a father teaching and training his children: *"Hear, my children, the instruction of a father, and give attention to know understanding; for I give you good doctrine: do not forsake my law. When I was my father's son, tender and the only one in the sight of my mother, he also taught me, and said to me: "Let your heart retain my words; keep my commands, and live'"* (Prov. 4:1–4). The Word also says, *My son, pay attention to my wisdom; lend your ear to my understanding, that you may preserve discretion, and your lips may keep knowledge* (Prov. 5:1–2).

No wonder the enemy has worked so hard to produce fatherless families. We know that if a statement is true, its converse is also true. Our children learn well from what we model, even if it is negative.

Unhealed areas between parents and children transmit sin. Pressure from a twisted influence will twist our perceptions. Our response to the ghosts of our past is up to us. We can deny that we are hurt or have issues. We can avoid facing our hurts and issues even though we know they are haunting us. We can endure the results and think there is no way out—*or we can choose to change.*[2]

Sometimes changing seems impossible, for we have "been this way" so long that we think we are "normal." However, biblical truth helps us see how to receive redemption and restoration.

Exodus 20:5–6 says, *"You shall not bow down to [other gods] nor serve them. For I, the LORD your God, am a jealous God, **visiting** the **iniquity** of the fathers upon the children to the third and fourth generations of those who hate Me, but showing mercy to thousands, to those who love Me and keep My commandments."*

The Hebrew word for *visiting* is *paqad*. This word is translated many ways in English but generally paints a picture of "rulers or authority figures [parents, for example] who so influence or pressure those under them that they are turned or twisted in their gifts." In other words, everything parents do *counts* in the life of their child. Furthermore, the word for *iniquity* comes from the same root that translates *wicked*, and indicates "something twisted or bent." Therefore, we can see that our upbringing can establish roots in us that cause the reproduction of twisted, rather than healthy, fruit.

Jesus went to the cross for our most deeply hidden, untold, or unrecognized wounds. A bruise is a wound under our skin where blood rushes to bring healing. Isaiah 53:6 says, *"He was bruised for our iniquities."* Thus no hurt could ever exist in us that Jesus has not already made healing provision for, regardless of how badly the hurt has twisted us or how long or deep its wound.

We always have the choice either to accept or reject the healing Jesus paid for: we can deny we have a problem and need to change; we can stay "in fear" and avoid confronting the problem with the truth; we can just endure the situation year after year; or *we can change*. Healing is always available.[3]

If either a parent or a child is walking in offense to the other, or if a parent is offended at someone outside the family, the defilement will be transmitted and bring poison into all of the relationships.

A young person most likely will make an inner vow such as, *When I grow up I am never going to* _____. This vow will control and come back up in the person, bearing terrible fruit.

Anytime we lift up ourselves in pride to judge another person, we will be judged by the same measure. The standard of judgment we apply to others will apply to us, and we will suffer the same condemnation. It will repeat itself in our circumstances and in our hearts until we repent and let go of that judgment.

Holding on to unforgiveness has the same consequences. We will find ourselves doing the very thing that has offended us. It's as if the attitude or behavior becomes our model, filed away for future use. Only truth and repentance heals (see Matt. 7:1).

Louis and I learned about "soul ties" from a friend who reported good results while praying for his father. The older gentleman was suffering physical and mental turmoil. The son discovered Proverbs 5:22 that says, *His own iniquities entrap the wicked man, and he is caught in the cords of his sin.* Being well aware of his father's sinful life, the son prayed and broke the ties between his father and all of his adulterous partners. God completely delivered his father.

Further research in God's Word yielded other affirming direction for us to use when ministering to those who had made inner vows or cast judgments, or who had unforgiveness or soul ties. Psalm 7:15–16 gives a clear picture of what happens when we remain in sin: *He who digs a hole and scoops it out, **falls into the pit he has made**. The trouble he causes recoils on himself; his violence comes down on his own head"* (NIV). Psalm 88 gives another distinct image: *For my soul is full of troubles, and my life draws near to the grave. I am counted with those who go **down to the pit**; I am like a man who has no strength. Shall Your lovingkindness be declared in the grave? Or Your faithfulness in the place of destruction?* (vv. 3–4, 11).

Other scriptures support the existence of soul ties and tell what to do about them. Louis and I discovered this reference: *"And they had as king over them the angel of the bottomless pit, whose name in Hebrew is **Abaddon**, but in Greek he has the name **Apollyon**"* (Rev. 9:11). According to *Strong's Concordance*, these names mean "destruction" or "destroyer."[4] We could see we'd found a great weapon for deliverance in using this tool, so we began to bind up the spirit of Abaddon and ask the angels to rescue the broken soul fragments from the pit and restore them to their rightful home. We also used Psalm 23:3 as a promise to restore souls.

We've seen hundreds of people set free from all types of sinful bondage they'd fallen prey to through ungodly connections. The sin these precious ones had participated in had caused their souls to fragment. This tool of binding and loosing works extremely efficiently where there has been sexual sin. Thank God, through His Word, He provides deliverance from the pit where our soul fragments are entrapped!

We have also been able to reverse the destroying effects in people who have partnered in crime and had negative agreement in their families. *Will evildoers never learn—*

those who devour my people as men eat bread and who do not call on the LORD? (Psalms 14:4 NIV).

One biblical example of crime and negative familial agreement is the Genesis 34 account of the prince of Shechem defiling Jacob's daughter, Dinah.

> And Dinah the daughter of Leah, which she bare unto Jacob, went out to see the daughters of the land. And when Shechem the son of Hamor the Hivite, prince of the country, saw her, he took her, and lay with her, and defiled her. And his soul clave unto Dinah the daughter of Jacob, and he loved the damsel, and spake kindly unto the damsel. And Shechem spake unto his father Hamor, saying, Get me this damsel to wife.
>
> And Jacob heard that he had defiled Dinah his daughter: now his sons were with his cattle in the field: and Jacob held his peace until they were come (1–5 KJV).

At first this story sounds like it could have a good outcome, but Dinah's brothers were so angry that they went behind their father's back and murdered all the men in the town.

Sin without repentance and cleansing will defile families for generations. The families of the Bible had more than their share of dysfunction. King David's family was another example. Many Bible scholars think David's older brothers dishonored him because he had a different mother than they did, a mother from a relationship outside Jesse's marriage. This extra-marital connection could account for David's bent toward multiple sexual relationships. He fathered a number of children from several wives. It appears he would only have one, or at most two, babies with a wife and then would move on to another woman. After the stunning episode of acquiring Bathsheba as his wife, he endured the tragic loss of their first child, conceived in adultery. Nonetheless, David and Bathsheba seemed to have had a lengthy marriage. Their next son was Solomon, whom they carefully trained to be king, and more children followed.

We see the fruit of this generational pattern in the lives of David's older children. One son raped his half-sister and was killed by her full brother. David apparently never communicated about the incident with any of those involved. This lack of communication resulted in disappointment, resentment, anger, withdrawal, frustration, murder, and rebellion. One of the brothers lived in exile for a while, and he later tried to wrest the kingdom from his father.

The enemy draws us into disconnecting from the Lord and finding other things to worship. The Lord is very clear that we are to put him *first* and *only*. We cooperate in the enemy's strategies by finding many other things to be "god" to us.

> "Therefore say to the house of Israel, 'Thus says the Lord GOD: "Repent, turn away from your idols, and turn your faces away from all your abominations. For anyone of the house of Israel, or of the strangers who dwell in Israel, who separates himself from Me and sets up his idols in his heart and puts before him what causes him to stumble into iniquity, then comes to a prophet to inquire of him concerning Me, I the LORD will answer him by Myself."'" (Ezek. 14:6–7).

Several years ago the word of the Lord came to me, saying, "Choosing your perception of 'reality'—believing the power of the circumstances—rather that believing My Word is idolatry." This word was very impacting.

We are all guilty of looking at our circumstances and getting stuck there. We are to look beyond what we see to what God says about the problem. He always has an answer and the means to cause it to come to be.

When the Lord spoke to me, He had already brought a lot of healing and correction to me through helping me recognize my own pride, which means I had been making myself my god. He said, "Carol, how you see things is not always how they are." The scripture He used was Proverbs 12:15: *The way of a fool is right in his own eyes.*

The Masonic order, fraternities, sororities, and all other "secret" societies are men's and women's efforts to bless themselves through social connections. Some of these societies are elaborate, some simple; some are based on ambition, some on a common hatred (e.g., the KKK). They all believe their particular group gives them an extra "edge" for favor or privilege. Sometimes this type of structure is commonly referred to as the "good-ol'-boy" system—advancement, not because of *what* you know, but because of *whom* you know. The promise of money and/or influence works the same way; its structure operates from a demonic base and includes a great deal of control and manipulation—favors done in return for favors given.

The good-ol'-boy system is a counterfeit system—kingdom connection is God's system because kingdom connection manifests His *glory*. Covenants and family, on earth, are legitimate connections, and this is why the enemy hates them so much.

We can fall into many traps that "help us" put someone or something ahead of our loving Father. Most of these snares trace back to keeping old attitudes from the self life where we lived before we met the Lord. He will constantly help us see and correct these old thought habits.

"I have not spoken in secret, in a dark place of the earth; I did not say to the seed of Jacob, 'Seek Me in vain'; I, the LORD, speak righteousness, I declare things that are right" (Isa. 45:19). When divisions and destructions exist in relationships, the Lord always has a specific answer to bring unity and restoration. The Holy Spirit will direct us to the explanation we need to lead us in specific repentance and forgiveness. Our standard must be the truth of the Word. The fabric of our lives needs to contain a generous portion of the

thread of the blood so that we walk in peace with ourselves and all men.

Relationships

Relationship is about connection. We do not exist in a vacuum. We are made for connection because that is who God is—a divine relationship. The Trinity is a family. How else could He be love?

It is easy to see that relationship is the heart of God. The beginning structure of creation was a marriage (see Gen. 1:27, 2:22–24). Father called Israel His bride. Jesus portrayed Himself as the Bridegroom (see Matt. 9:15; John 3:29). We know we will celebrate the marriage of the Lamb at the end (see Rev. 19:7–9).

In 2 Corinthians 11:2, Paul says that God has betrothed us to one husband, Christ. Ephesians 5:21–33 gives us the beautiful description of marriage as a picture of Christ and the church.

If wounds have made us withdraw from others or isolate ourselves, this disconnection is an indication we need to receive Father's love. We need to be heart healthy for our marriages and other relationships to prosper. As we touch one another at a heart level, we really begin to know one another. As we honor, encourage, delight in, listen to, share with, and nurture each other, we "love one another."

In marriage, our connection to our spouse must be healthy and reflect the love of the Lord. We *respond* to one another because our spouse is a joy to us, and we are always finding new facets to appreciate.

Responding to our spouse in love is the opposite of loading our spouse with the *responsibility* to "make me happy." This dynamic is unhealthy—in fact, it's just as bad as loading ourselves with the responsibility of making our spouse happy. Taking *responsibility* for our spouse's happiness is burdensome. *Responding* to our spouse in love is spontaneous and joyful!

Marriage and family are a connection by blood. Holy matrimony is a covenant meant to be sealed with blood. Under God's direction, in the Hebrew culture a father guarded his daughter until she was given in marriage to her husband. Then she came into her husband's covenant with God, which was formed at his circumcision. Thus women and their children were always protected by covenant.

The Lord has our families planned ahead of time. The lineage of David is particularly interesting. This Hebrew family left Judea and then had many problems, including the death of all but one. Naomi, the remaining representative of the family, returned to Judea and brought back with her Ruth the Moabitess, who was destined to be in David's ancestry. Naomi then connected Ruth with Boaz because Naomi understood the family principles of the covenant.

As we connect with people in a healthy way through the love of Jesus, we have wholeness. Ephesians 2:19–22 says, *Now, therefore, you are no longer strangers and foreigners, but fellow citizens with the saints and members of the household of God, having been built on the foundation of the apostles and prophets, Jesus Christ Himself being the chief cornerstone, in whom the whole building, being fitted together, grows into a holy temple in the Lord, in whom you also are being built together for a dwelling place of God in the Spirit.* In this way, the whole body of Christ is smoothly connected, each person doing his or her part.

We see other examples of healthy connections in the Word. In 1 Samuel 18, Jonathan and David were covenant brothers in arms. In 1 Kings 19:19, Elijah calls Elisha to be his spiritual son. We see in 2 Kings 2 that Elisha follows Elijah faithfully to the end of his assignment and picks up Elijah's mantle to carry on the work with a double portion.

The Lord is continually bringing about divine connections to further His work on earth. We will each have many such connections, for long and short seasons, during our deployment here. We can validate one another when we are called alongside to help. Shared joy and laughter, as well as shared pain, connect us with people. Our emotions carry frequency and enable us to empathize with others. In times of trauma, we let down self-defense and connect with another's need.

In our day and time, great dysfunction exists in Father's design for relationships. Our culture has taken a wrong turn. It is as the prophet Hosea said:

Hear the word of the LORD, you children of Israel, for the LORD brings a charge against the inhabitants of the land:

"There is no truth or mercy or knowledge of God in the land. By swearing and lying, killing and stealing and committing adultery, they break all restraint, with bloodshed upon bloodshed. Therefore the land will mourn; and everyone who dwells there will waste away with the beasts of the field and the birds of the air; even the fish of the sea will be taken away.

"Now let no man contend, or rebuke another; for your people are like those who contend with the priest" (Hos. 4:1–4).

Even so, the Lord is well able to remove the hardness from our hearts as we turn back to Him. For instance, one time I was struggling with some insecurity issues. One of my favorite scriptures had always been Psalm 23, and I prayed it daily during that time. (I enjoyed the concept of the Lord, my shepherd, caring for me.) Then He opened up Hosea 4:16 to me: *For Israel has behaved stubbornly, like a stubborn heifer. How then should he expect to be fed and treated by the Lord like a lamb in a large pasture?* (AMPC). I quickly asked Him to show me where I was stubborn—and was shocked when He showed me how much I needed to repent for. So I renewed my mind and turned the other way! I am sure my whole family was vastly relieved.

When we receive correction, direction, or any other leading, it connects us with God's gift of grace. He likewise connects us with family, friends, teachers, and other precious ones as we pray for them.

Strong family connections cause us to be secure and teach us how to be comfortable. With healthy parent-child bonding, our emotional growth is steady. When our own need to be heard and understood is satisfied, we are able to respond to others freely. I recall that I was forty years old and sought counseling before I ever felt as if someone "heard" me. It was amazing to me what a fulfilling release that was. When we cannot trust that anyone will respond to our needs, we develop a deep distrust of all connections.

As children, many of us did not learn to express our feelings in a healthy way. We did not have the language to share what we were experiencing and were not "heard" when we did try to share. Often this meant we squelched strong feelings.

In a healthy family, our "free" connections teach us manners, delayed gratification, giving and receiving, and a balance of dependence and independence. We learn to manage stress levels and accept both failure and success. We can ask for help, say "I'm sorry," and maintain boundaries.

Trauma in a family situation disrupts our ability to learn these healthy skills. When we were children, if we saw adults blaming each other instead of taking responsibility for their own actions, we likely copied this model. We also probably copied patterns of withdrawal and denial.

Let's look at the Twenty-third Psalm I mentioned previously: *The LORD is my shepherd; I shall not want. He makes me to lie down in green pastures; He leads me beside the still waters. He restores my soul; He leads me in the paths of righteousness for His name's sake* (vv. 1–3). One of the chief things the Lord assures us of is His protection. He also portrays Himself as our provider. Thus He sets the model for husbands and fathers in families (see Eph. 3:15).

It is a great comfort to a single woman that He is husband. *"For your Maker is your husband, the LORD of hosts is His name; and your Redeemer is the Holy One of Israel; He is called the God of the whole earth"* (Isa. 54:5). When we study the roots of words, we find that *husband* signifies "one who takes care of."[1] The Lord wants to take care of us, as much as we need to be cared for!

Other scriptures depict the Father as a farmer and us as the fruit of His plantings. Jesus said in John 15, *"I am the true vine, and My Father is the vinedresser,"* and *"By this My Father is glorified, that you bear much fruit; so you will be My disciples"* (vv. 1, 8). God is patient and longsuffering with us, because He is growing us! We are not machines that need fixing, but organisms that grow. If we look at our marriage the same way He does, we see He has put us together to grow in Him and into His likeness. This view keeps us from trying to "fix" each other and rather to sow the best seed we have into the relationship. Father also gives us the seed to sow (see 2 Cor. 9:10).

At the same time, we can allow Him to grow us into the best spouse we can be by giving Him free reign to prune and weed us. *Therefore be patient, brethren, until the coming of the Lord. See how the farmer waits for the precious fruit of the earth, waiting patiently for it until it receives the early and latter rain. You also be patient. Establish your hearts, for the coming of the Lord is at hand* (James 5:7–8).

Leadership is a huge assignment for men. Most have not seen godly leadership modeled. As adults they find little training available to assist them in being good husbands and fathers. Many try to fit the lifestyle they had as singles into married life. Then, too, men tend to be prideful, so Father instructs them to humble themselves. Godly leadership carries responsibility, humility, and service.

Just as being humble is hard for many men, being a follower is difficult for many women. Most of them love to lead and think they "know better" than their husbands (and some-times even the Lord), so the Word tells wives to submit and adapt. This instruction may not be popular or "politically correct," but it is the biblical pattern. Jesus is the primary example of a submitted life. He only did and said what His Father said to do and say!

John 17:22 tells us that Jesus has given us the glory so that we may be one. Could this possibly mean we are going to need the presence and substance of the Lord with us and in us for our relationships to work right? Since the Lord has poured His love into us thorough the Holy Spirit (see Rom. 5:5), He has empowered us to love with His love. His pattern is clear in 1 Corinthians 13:4–8:

> Love endures long and is patient and kind; love never is envious nor boils over with jealousy, is not boastful or vainglorious, does not display itself haugh-tily.
>
> It is not conceited (arrogant and inflated with pride); it is not rude (unmannerly) and does not act un-becomingly. Love (God's love in us) does not insist on its own rights or its own way, for it is not self-seeking;

it is not touchy or fretful or resentful; it takes no account of the evil done to it [it pays no attention to a suffered wrong].

It does not rejoice at injustice and unrighteousness, but rejoices when right and truth prevail.

Love bears up under anything and everything that comes, is ever ready to believe the best of every person, its hopes are fadeless under all circumstances, and it endures everything [without weakening].

Love never fails [never fades out or becomes obsolete or comes to an end] (AMPC).

Note particularly that love doesn't keep lists of wrongs done. It is quick to forgive and let go of hurts and disappointments. Practicing this type of love will work wonderful change in our lives.

I like to think of marriage as a treasure hunt. Father, the master designer, has placed innumerable gifts and graces in each one of us. Some gifts are visible to all. Others are only to be discovered by our spouse. This search for the treasure in each other and the appreciation for it is a life-long blessing. We will always be looking for and finding new things, and can bring out and polish up ones we have seen before.

We are guardians of these treasures, not competitors with them. We must protect those treasures that are fragile and only for our eyes.

To do this, we can ask Father to open our eyes to see past the obvious. If we are motivated by the His love, He will show us His gifts in others.

Most of us haven't even come to terms with the truth that He treasures *us*! His covenant of blessing and grace brings us into a safe place. We can only relax and open ourselves to healing if we know we are not at risk when we are vulnerable. Our assignment of reconciliation means we are to help each other heal. *Brethren, if a man is overtaken in any trespass, you who are spiritual restore such a one in a spirit of gentleness, considering yourself lest you also be tempted* (Gal. 6:1–2). When we see that we are treasured, it helps us see others as treasures too.

God's whole purpose is to restore us to Himself. Salvation is not just a ticket to heaven or even about just being forgiven. Those benefits are only the beginning. He wants to restore total wholeness, love, and dominion to us. Look at this concept from heaven's viewpoint: *"You have seen what I did to the Egyptians, and how I bore you on eagles' wings and brought you to Myself. Now therefore, if you will indeed obey My voice and keep My covenant, then you shall be a special treasure to Me above all people; for all the earth is Mine"* (Ex. 19:4–6).

Many times Scripture reminds us the Lord values us as a treasure or special inheritance:

"Also today the LORD has proclaimed you to be *His special people*, just as He promised you, that you should keep all His commandments, and that He will set you *high above all nations* which He has made, in praise, in name, and in honor, and that you may be *a holy people* to the LORD your God, just as He has spoken" (Deut. 26:18–19).

You shall also be *a crown of glory* in the hand of the LORD, and *a royal diadem* in the hand of your God (Isa. 62:3).

Then those who feared the LORD spoke to one another, and the LORD listened and heard them; so a book of remembrance was written before Him for those who fear the LORD and who meditate on His name.

"They shall be Mine," says the LORD of hosts, "on the day that I make them *My jewels*. And I will spare them as a man spares his own son who serves him" (Mal. 3:16–17).

Coming to Him as to a living stone, rejected indeed by men, but chosen by God and precious, you also, as *living stones*, are being built up a spiritual house, a holy priesthood, to offer up spiritual sacrifices acceptable to God through Jesus Christ (1 Pet. 2:4–5).

As I was studying these verses, the Lord said, "I see you as sparkling, radiant jewels!" If He sees us that way, we can see others that way!

Recently I heard a wife say that as she and her husband had prayed for the healing of their marriage, they discovered they also needed to thank the Lord their *real* connection was through Jesus Christ. Wow!

For the enemy to work so hard in trying to establish negative connections, God's connections must bring *real* life. Connection *in Him* is true covenant connection. Asking Him to purify our connections (marital or otherwise) *in Him* is perhaps one of the greatest keys to healing the connections.

As we come into fellowship with each other, knowing we are in Him, all our interactions will take on a new level of joy.

By faith we understand that the worlds were framed by the word of God, so that the things which are seen were not made of things which are visible (Heb. 11:3). In like fashion, we "frame" our relationships by the words we speak about them. This word *frame* in Greek is *katartizo*, which *Strong's* defines as "to arrange, set in order, equip, adjust, complete what is lacking, make fully ready, repair, prepare."[2] What grace we are given to change our world—and our relationships—by the words we speak!

Body Connections

Made in the image of God, we are three-part beings. First Thessalonians 5:23 gives us the correct order of these three parts: *Now may the God of peace Himself sanctify you completely; and may your whole **spirit, soul, and body** be preserved blameless at the coming of our Lord Jesus Christ.* For the purpose of our study on connections, I will discuss these parts in reverse order. Let's look at *body connections* first.

Physical touch transmits an amazing power. Many connections, good and bad, on many levels, can occur when hands and bodies touch.

A major portion of biblical doctrine—including anointing, healing, and gifts—transfers through, or is imparted by, touch. Hebrews 6:1–3, which enumerates the fundamental principles of Christianity, refers to this impartation: *Therefore, leaving the discussion of the elementary principles of Christ, let us go on to perfection, not laying again the foundation of repentance from dead works and of faith toward God, of the doctrine of baptisms, of **laying on of hands**, of resurrection of the dead, and of eternal judgment.*

A touch is also effective when directed by the Lord.

We were sharing at a meeting in California years ago in the 1980s. As we ministered to individuals in the class, a woman came forward for a "Mommy and Daddy hug." She'd been using a walker, but she left it at the altar that day. The touch of the Lord healed her! We were later told the friend who had brought her had touched her on the shoulder with the compassion of Jesus flowing out to her throughout the meeting. (While the report of pain from an injury to your finger travels to your brain at 3.5 mph, the report of a hug speeds along at 35 mph.) We also learned she was on the board of the National Multiple Sclerosis Society and had been suffering MS for years.

The Old Testament provides a number of other references to touch. Second Kings 13:20–21 says, *Then Elisha died, and they buried him. And the raiding bands from Moab invaded the land in the spring of the year. So it was, as they were burying a man, that suddenly they spied a band of raiders; and they put the man in the tomb of Elisha; and when the man was let down and touched the bones of Elisha, he revived and stood on his feet.* What an astounding account of the life-giving power transmitted through touch! On the other hand, Chronicles 16:22 warns, *"Do not touch My anointed ones, and do My prophets no harm."* From these two passages, we see that life can be imparted where the Lord is present and harm can come where malevolent intent exists.

The prophet Isaiah reported a vision he received: *Then one of the seraphim flew to me, having in his hand a live coal which he had taken with the tongs from the altar. And he touched my mouth with it, and said: "Behold, this has touched your lips; your iniquity is taken away, and your sin purged"* (Isa. 6:6–7). Daniel also experienced a heavenly touch in a vision: *Now, as he was speaking with me, I was in a deep sleep with my face to the ground; but he touched me, and stood me upright* (Dan. 8:18). In these passages we see cleansing and strength imparted.

The Scriptures also recognize the harm of negative touch and give many cautions about touching things that are dead or "defiled." In the book of Numbers, the priests were taught to avoid anything "unclean" and how be cleansed from such contact.

The Pharisees of Jesus' day thought He should avoid anyone who was defiled, or unclean. Luke 7 portrays the story of the woman who approached Jesus when He was attending a dinner at a Pharisee's home:

Then one of the Pharisees asked Him to eat with him. And He went to the Pharisee's house, and sat down to eat. And behold, a woman in the city who was a sinner, when she knew that Jesus sat at the table in the Pharisee's house, brought an alabaster flask of fragrant oil, and stood at His feet behind Him weeping; and she began to wash His feet with her tears, and wiped them with the hair of her head; and *she kissed His feet and anointed them* with the fragrant oil. Now when the Pharisee who had invited Him saw this, he spoke to himself, saying, "This Man, if He were a prophet, would know who and what manner of woman this is *who is touching Him,* for she is a sinner."

And Jesus answered and said to him, "Simon, I have something to say to you."

So he said, "Teacher, say it."

"There was a certain creditor who had two debtors. One owed five hundred denarii, and the other fifty. And when they had nothing with which to repay, he freely forgave them both. Tell Me, therefore, which of them will love him more?"

Simon answered and said, "I suppose the one whom he forgave more."

And He said to him, "You have rightly judged." Then He turned to the woman and said to Simon, "Do you see this woman? I entered your house; you gave Me no water for My feet, but she has washed My feet with her tears and wiped them with the hair of her head. You gave Me no kiss, but this woman has not ceased to *kiss My feet* since the time I came in. You did not anoint My head with oil, but this woman has *anointed My feet* with fragrant oil. Therefore I say to you, her sins, which are many, are forgiven, *for she loved much*. But to whom little is forgiven, the same loves little."

Then He said to her, "Your sins are forgiven" (Luke 7:36–48).

When the woman washed Jesus' feet with her tears and dried them with her hair, Simon, the host, was incensed, because she had a "reputation." His view was that this woman's touch made Jesus unclean. Jesus had a totally different view than the Pharisee of what happened when an un-clean person touched Him. Jesus reversed the defilement this woman carried. He told Simon that her touch could not bring Him down but, rather, that her love and repentance connected her to His grace, cleansing her and setting her free. He then contrasted her devoted, loving actions with the Pharisee's pride and lack of compassion in his hosting—very little love there!

Earlier we referenced 1 Corinthians 13:6, *Love keeps no record of a suffered wrong.* It's important to note that even though Jesus commands us to forgive and not keep a record of a wrong suffered, the human body can keep memories of hurts at the cellular level. The body is a unified whole, and when one part hurts, it affects the rest. (This concept applies to the body of Christ as well: when one part hurts, it causes pain in the rest.) Likewise, emotional wounds affect the physical body, and often vice versa.

One time when I was meditating on what the Lord was showing me about cell memory, I "saw" a small wire of negative memory working its way in between large cables of truth from God. The enemy works this way to keep us "connected" to old wounds.

Research shows that memories are retained at the cellular level in the belly and in the heart muscle, as well as in the brain. These memories keep people connected with trauma, which explains many issues related to depression and emotional instability.[1]

Our ministry has encountered more than one person who struggled with carrying too much weight. In many instances, when these people learned to let go of hurts and to forgive others and themselves, the weight disappeared.

How wonderful that we have Jesus' example of using the powerful touch of compassion and grace to heal. *Touch* in the Greek is *haptomi,* and means "to hold, touch, embrace."[2] As Jesus lovingly touched and embraced people, they received healing. Many instances in Scripture verify this truth. Here are only a few:

Then Jesus put out His hand and touched him, saying, "I am willing; be cleansed." Immediately his leprosy was cleansed" (Matt. 8:3).

Now when Jesus had come into Peter's house, He saw his wife's mother lying sick with a fever. So He touched her hand, and the fever left her. And she arose and served them (Matt. 8:14–15).

Others heard what His touch could do and came expecting to receive from Him:

And suddenly, a woman who had a flow of blood for twelve years came from behind and touched the hem of His garment. For she said to herself, "If only I may touch His garment, I shall be made well." But Jesus turned around, and when He saw her He said, "Be of good cheer, daughter; your faith has made you well." And the woman was made well from that hour" (Matt. 9:20–22).

Then He touched their eyes, saying, "According to your faith let it be to you" (Matt. 9:29).

And when the men of that place recognized Him, they sent out into all that surrounding region, brought to Him all who were sick, and begged Him that they might only touch the hem of His garment. And as many as touched it were made perfectly well (Matt. 14:35–36).

The people recognized Jesus' touch had the power of blessing in it. He demonstrated this truth in many ways. His "blessing touch" multiplied food:

And when He had taken the five loaves and the two fish, He looked up to heaven, blessed and broke the loaves, and gave them to His disciples to set before them; and the two fish He divided among them all (Mark 6:41–42).

Parents brought their children to receive the blessing touch:

Then they brought little children to Him, that He might touch them; but the disciples rebuked those who brought them. But when Jesus saw it, He was greatly displeased and said to them, "Let the little children come to Me, and do not forbid them; for of such is the kingdom of God. Assuredly, I say to you, whoever does not receive the kingdom of God as a little child will by no means enter it." And He took them up in His arms, laid His hands on them, and blessed them (Mark 10:13–16).

We can see how Father intended touch connections to be a mighty blessing in the earth. We can honor His intention by making our touches to others a love gift from Him. Because we house the presence of the Lord, we do not need to fear a negative touch. This type of touch can happen in crowds and other ways, some on purpose and some not. Whether bumps or germs, we need not fear. His presence in us is greater than any assignment the enemy sends against us.

We are to follow Jesus' example of using touch to bless others, never to harm. One thing the Lord instructed me to do is to speak a blessing over babies. I do this in grocery stores and wherever I go, as the Lord leads. I have only been refused once when I offered this blessing. We should stop thinking of ourselves and obey the Lord's prompting to reach out and bless others. A hug, a pat, a friendly touch can warm the heart of someone who is hurting.

The Lord is well able to heal us from the effects of any negative touches we may have experienced. Many people carry trauma from having witnessed or been victims of domestic violence. In fact, studies prove that when children even see or hear this kind of negativity, it traumatizes them. Fear penetrates deeply into their tender spirits and souls.[3]

Anyone who has suffered or witnessed violence—from the child in a domestic situation to the soldier on a battle-field—experiences trauma that registers in the physical body. Fear and trauma cause ongoing tensions that will last a lifetime unless the person's heart is healed. But a healed heart frees the body from the negative effects.

I found three scriptures that indicate a principle a principle the enemy uses to keep people bound so that they do not recognize the root of their issues. Exodus 20:19 and Romans 8:15 are summarized in Hebrews 2:15: *And release those who through fear of death were all their lifetime subject to bondage.* Fear of death is quite common and often begins when a person experiences physical pain. This fear opens the door to other traumas.

Many of us have experienced various sorts of pain through our relationships. Especially when the same pattern of pain repeats, it can be a flag to let us know that a root issue requires healing. So we see that pain can be a help to us.

Looking unto Jesus, the author and finisher of our faith, who for the joy that was set before Him endured the cross, despising the shame, and has sat down at the right hand of the throne of God (Heb. 12:2).

Our Master endured an enormous amount of pain to purchase our freedom from the sin nature and all of the corruption it brought into our world. We will never have as much pain to suffer as He did. Can we see pain as a positive challenge in our lives, one that keeps us from ignoring trouble?

Why do you think there is such pain in broken relationships? Does it hurt your heart when a marriage breaks apart, or someone dies and the person's family is bereft? How does this pain look from Father's perspective? What can we learn from pain?

I used to run from pain as hard as I could. Then several years ago, I read Dr. Paul Brand's book *Pain: The Gift Nobody Wants*. Dr. Brand was raised in India by missionary parents. After becoming a physician, he returned to India and spent many years caring for lepers. He and his team discovered that neuropathy, or nerve damage, causes lepers to lose parts of their bodies. A wound would occur and pain couldn't register. Because of subsequent infection, the lepers would lose a toe, a finger, an ear, or a foot—all because they could not feel pain! Dr. Brand later worked in the USA with diabetics who suffer the same kind of neuropathy.[4]

Pain locates our heart issues. In trying to avoid pain, have you ever created more pain? I certainly have. Change is often painful. The only way to evaluate our choices is by seeing them from Father's viewpoint! Does our pain echo His?

The Bible is about Father's story of painful loss and what He is doing to win back His rebellious, lost love. All through the Old Testament, He compares His relationship with Israel to a marriage. In many Scriptures He refers to her rebellion as adultery and unfaithfulness. He also speaks of His heart to draw her back to Himself! Does our pain echo His? Ezekiel 16 and the book of Hosea vividly picture Father's dramatic wooing of and subsequent marriage to Israel, along with her unfaithfulness to Him and His forgiveness and restoration for her. Redemption and restoration are always available.

John the Baptist described Jesus as the Bridegroom, and Jesus referred to Himself that way. Paul said he betrothed us (the church) to Christ (see 2 Corinthians 11:2) and often used the marriage relationship as an example for Christ and the church.

The pain we experience in our daily relationships should send us directly to Father's arms for wisdom and healing. He alone can show us our root issues and heal our deepest wounds. Without the pain, we would never know there was something wrong we needed to deal with. What a blessing to feel pain! Only our wonderful Creator would equip us so thoroughly!

Soul Connections

Like many other of Father's designs, the "soul" of man is made up of three parts. These are the mind, the will, and the emotions. Our *mind* receives, collects, and sorts information, instructing our body how to function. Our *will* takes information and decides what our response should be. Our *emotions* respond with feelings that move us to act, positively or negatively.

Because we live in a noisy, information-saturated world, we have an enormous amount of data coming at us all the time. Sound bombards our ears, light flashes toward our eyes, and fragrances and tastes of all kinds are available to us. Music touches us in amazing ways and can manipulate our emotions. All of this data can affect us mentally, volitionally, and emotionally.

God designed the soul to be the connector between the spirit and the body, or physical world. At the fall, the human spirit lost its connection to God and left the soul in leadership. After we are born again, we have to *retrain our soul* to yield to our regenerated spirit.

Let's look at how our mind, our world view, or the "mental part of our soul" works. How we have been trained, purposely or accidentally, to interpret the world around us makes a huge difference in how we live. Of course, our first impressions come through our family, and these beliefs set the stage for the rest of our lives.

The information and misinformation that comes through our soul greatly affects our relationships. Often, we have to take numerous biblical concepts in good faith, because we have never seen them lived out. One of these concepts is that "the connections we make with other people affect our soul's health."

Heart Menders has ministered for years in breaking negative soul ties. (See chapter 3 for a discussion of this subject.) One of the most obvious ways we see negative soul ties play out is in generational sin passed down through family lines. Once the enemy has trapped someone in a sin such as sexual immorality, greed, deceit, or idolatry, the seed keeps producing. The same pattern can, and usually will, ravage that person's descendants for decades and centuries.

The Lord pulled no punches in telling the stories of His chosen family, Israel—certainly a family that had more than its share of wounded hearts. This truth gives us hope that our family, too, can survive and overcome.

We still suffer today from the sibling rivalry of Abraham's sons. Isaac didn't marry until after Sarah died. The Genesis account tells us that when he, at age forty, married Rebekah (a teenage bride who had left home and family to become his wife), he took her to his mother's tent and "was comforted after his mother's death"! Do you think that was a good way to start a marriage?

It's not surprising that, sixty years later, we find Rebekah bitter toward life. She had been married twenty years before she bore her twin sons, Esau and Jacob, and they were nearly forty when Jacob left home. She never saw this favorite son again. The bitterness traces through her sons and daughters-in-law's lineage, manifesting in particular in the rivalry of Jacob's sons.

As we have already discussed, sexual sin haunted David's family and produced negative outcomes. Another result of this sin was the destruction of David's relationship with one of his foremost advisors, Ahithophel, who joined Absalom's rebellion against David. If we trace the biblical references to Ahithophel, we discover he was Bathsheba's grandfather. This connection indicates his long-buried wound over her disgrace, which turned him against his own great-grandson, Solomon, the designated crown prince. This snare of sexual sin opened the door for Solomon to have many wives and be drawn into idolatry by them.

Because of His covenant with Israel, the Lord was still able to work with these people to bring about His plan. In fact, David had amazing revelation of the mercy of God: *He brought them out of darkness and the shadow of death, and broke their chains in pieces. Oh, that men would give thanks to the LORD for His goodness, and for His wonderful works to the children of men!"* (Psalms 107:14–15).

The way parents deal with their children has far-reaching effects. Pastors rarely teach about the sin of offense, but Scripture tells us that taking offense is a destructive sin. If either a parent or a child is carrying an offense, it will cause snarls of judgment and unforgiveness. A child will often file the parental "model" of holding on to an offense, only to pull the file out at a later date and follow the model unconsciously.

Great power is released when two or more people agree on anything. Agreement involves both the mind and the will.

Numerous scriptures bear this truth out. Perhaps the most famous example in scripture of the power of agreement is God's intervention at the Tower of Babel so that the people could not communicate (see Gen. 11). Once they could no longer agree, they lost all power. Another well-known reference to agreement is the prophet Amos's question, *"Can two walk together, unless they are agreed?"* (Amos 3:3).

The Old Testament stipulated that two people had to agree on an accusation before it carried any weight. The Word contains many references to this principle, one of which is Deuteronomy 19:15: *"One witness shall not rise against a man concerning any iniquity or any sin that he commits; by the mouth of two or three witnesses the matter shall be established."* Such agreement can work in positive or negative ways.

The Bible gives us a wonderful promise when we apply the principle of agreement in the right way: *"Again I say to you that if two of you agree on earth concerning anything that they ask, it will be done for them by My Father in heaven"* (Matt. 18:19). Agreement yields an enormous amount of spiritual power. So anytime we agree with someone about an issue, we should know what the foundation of our agreement is. Are we are basing our agreement on the Word or on mere human thought and motive? This question especially applies to prayer requests.

We can avoid many problems if, daily and in every relationship, we set aside strife and find areas of agreement. To do so is particularly vital when there is a lot at stake. *Agree with your adversary quickly, while you are on the way with him, lest your adversary deliver you to the judge, the judge hand you over to the officer, and you be thrown into prison* (Matt. 5:25–26). The breakdown of communication causes great heartache.

Scripture affirms that the Lord was in perfect agreement with the Father to accomplish His purposes. Every part of Jesus' earthly assignment was in accord with the Father's divine plan. *It is also written in your law that the testimony of two men is true. I am One who bears witness of Myself, and the Father who sent Me bears witness of Me* (John 8:17).

Although not appreciated in our day, Father's use of covenant agreement is very powerful in accomplishing all it promises. In Abram's day, people were familiar with covenant because it was already established in human culture to demonstrate a life-or-death agreement. When God backed

His promises to Abram with a covenant, it sealed for Abram that the promises of children and land were certain. God renewed this covenant with succeeding generations since the promise was forever.

David and Jonathan made a covenant of friendship that was greater than Jonathan's future right to the throne (see 1 Sam. 18). David honored this covenant by caring for Jonathan's crippled son, Mephibosheth (see 2 Sam. 9).

Elisha's service to Elijah became a covenant that bound them so together that Elisha saw Elijah carried to heaven and received a double anointing.

Everything Father plans for us and the earth will come into alignment with His will. First John 5:8 says, *There are three that bear witness on earth: the Spirit, the water, and the blood; and these three agree as one.*

Unfortunately, the devil often gets more agreement for sin and darkness than the Lord does for His people to love and honor His Word!

Every scriptural principle works both ways. There is power in agreement for negative outcomes as well as for positive. We have to choose judiciously whom we agree with and what we agree about. So much of our general conversation is about other people and their problems and faults. It has been said that small-minded people talk about others, average people talk about things, and wise people talk about ideas. We must focus on situations with a view from above, as Colossians 3:1–2 says. When we agree with someone about others in a negative way, our words carry the wrong kind of power.

When I was growing up, I heard some of my aunts speak negatively about their husbands. This hurt my heart, because I liked my uncles. I decided then and there, when I grew up, I would not speak negatively about my husband. Before Louis and I came to the Lord, my children were teens and our family was struggling to survive. My older daughter was very angry toward her father. She would try to get me to say bad things about him and agree with her. I would not do so, and that made her even angrier. Later, when we learned some of these spiritual laws, she told me she believed our amazing healing was due in part to the Lord's honoring my commitment only to speak well of my husband.

When we face problems, we must objectively seek God's counsel. We should never seek sympathy for our point of view. Our words should always agree with Father's heart. Paul tells us in Ephesians 5:6–8, *Let no one deceive you with empty words, for because of these things the wrath of God comes upon the sons of disobedience. Therefore do not be partakers with them. For you were once darkness, but now you are light in the Lord. Walk as children of light.*

In the Old Testament, we repeatedly see incidents where the Israelites spoke negatively about themselves, opening the door to the enemy. Several times they told Moses, "We will die in this desert," and so finally the Lord gave them what they said. The prophet Isaiah said, *Because you have said, "We have made a covenant with death, and with Sheol we are in agreement. When the overflowing scourge passes through, it will not come to us, for we have made lies our refuge, and under falsehood we have hidden ourselves."* . . . *When the overflowing scourge passes through, then you will be trampled down by it* (Isa. 28:15, 18).

When we speak Father's words, He carries them out. When we speak negative words, we authorize the enemy to work. *And what agreement has the temple of God with idols? For you are the temple of the living God* (2 Cor. 6:16).

Where the mind leads, the will follows. We make choices based on the information our mind and other voices speak to us. However, we can choose what we think! Our mind is *our* mind, and we have authority to reject those things that are not of God. Paul tells us that we are to have the mind of Christ (see Phil. 2:5). The Bible instructs us to renew our minds, and we must purposefully do this. I have heard it said, and totally agree, that if we say we love Jesus and don't love Him enough to renew our minds, then we don't love Him!

We have to train our wills to choose only what the Lord directs. If we are used to flying all over the place with our choices, we will have to rein them in and direct them by the Word. Therefore, it is essential to know the Word so that we can retrain ourselves.

Some of the issues embedded in our soul cause us to be drawn to others who "match our pattern," often in the negative sense. For example, a person with a "victim" wound is very likely to be drawn to someone with a "predator" pattern. This type of negative patterning repeats itself endlessly. Healthy people are likewise drawn to healthy people.

Our emotions follow along behind our minds and wills like a puppy's tail follows him. Our feelings are not our guide! So many people give their emotions complete rule. People ask others how they *feel* about something far more than they ask them what they think or believe. This is tragic.

Sometimes what seems like a tragedy to us leads to a "glory story" for the Lord. The servant girl to Naaman's wife was a captive slave who had been carried away to Aram from her home in Israel. Yet she had enough grace in her heart to have compassion on her master, Naaman, and recommend that he could be healed by God's prophet, Elisha. Naaman almost missed his healing because of his emotional reaction. But in the end, he did humbly obey, was healed, and then committed his life to Jehovah for the rest of his days (see 2 Kings 5).

Our emotions are a gift from God. With them, we express joy and thanksgiving! Joy should be our thermostat to show how close we are to the Lord. We can quickly enter into praise because we are ever close to Him. Our born-again spirit can retrain our mind, will, and emotions to follow the Holy Spirit's leadings.

Nevertheless, the enemy wants to sow his negative seed into us through this avenue of "feelings." He sows emotions such as disappointment, despair, and fear, and we think these are ours! We never have to receive any of these feelings! Our situation in life does not determine our level of joy. We do not judge our identity or position by circumstances.

A spirit of grief and sadness is just that—a spirit—and not from God. No one who is rejoicing in the love of the Lord can stay depressed!

Only truth and repentance bring us true joy! The measure of our mindset, our choices, and our feelings must be the truth of the Word.

Spirit Connections

The spirit part of us is the chief part of our triune being. We *are* spirit, we have a soul, and we live in a body. From birth, we have a human spirit that gives us life, connects us with other people, and seeks to worship. With the new birth, our spirit is reborn and reconnected to the Lord.

How do we recognize our connection to the Lord and each other? Through our spirits. Our spirits are the vehicle for truly bonding with one another.

We recognize a blessing when we sense that "uplift of heart" that tells us, *This is a great thing!* Our heavenly Father is the true source of all blessings. He manifests them in various ways, both spiritual and natural. A healing that manifests, instantly or over time, is a blessing from the Healer. We might call all of the amazing ways the Lord meets our needs miraculous—but whether we consider them miracles or not, all are blessings, be they large or small.

Relationship connections that enrich, inspire, or comfort us are actual blessings from the Lord, poured out to us through other people. The opposite is also true: God also uses us as a channel for pouring His blessings out to others through our relationship with them. Loving one another in an honoring way is a precious gift from the Lord.

Years ago, I read a fictional story by Isaac Asimov that told of a space exploration venture in which a planet was discovered that was thought to have had no life form. On the way back to earth, a stowaway appeared in the spacecraft. This being, who had been the sole living entity on that planet, was invisible to humans. The being could hardly wait to get to earth to make all of humanity into creatures of his kind. However, he had inadvertently placed himself on the landing gear that would crush him when the ship landed.

The story was thought provoking. Human beings have a great resistance to losing their individuality.

So many people keep their hearts closed because they fear they will "lose themselves" in an intimate relationship. Or they separate from others over issues when they believe they are right and the other person wrong. Many stay in an unhealthy relationship because they fear the consequences of disconnection. They will not stand up and tell the truth because they are afraid of rejection, a major way of becoming disconnected.

We see this pattern of fear in the Bible when the Pharisees were investigating the healing of the man born blind. His parents would not affirm his amazing healing. *They said this [that they don't know what had happened to make him see, or who had done it] in fear of the Jewish leaders who had announced that anyone saying Jesus was the Messiah would be excommunicated* (John 9:22–23 TLB).

Only the Lord can connect us in a way that brings unity and still makes us unique in our identity. The Lord holds us each special and individual, yet can unite our spirits as one. Otherwise, why would our Master have prayed the following prayer in John 17:20–23?

"I do not pray for these alone, but also for those who will believe in Me through their word; that they all may be one, as You, Father, are in Me, and I in You; that they also may be one in Us, that the world may believe that You sent Me. And the glory which You gave Me I have given them, that they may be one just as We are one: I in them, and You in Me; that they may be made perfect in one, and that the world may know that You have sent Me, and have loved them as You have loved Me."

We see here again that the glory is a factor in bringing us together. The substance of His presence in each of us draws us to one another. Just as we all have flesh, blood, and bone, so we all have access to the Lord's glory. In fact, His light in us peeks though and is often acknowledged in the earth. After we leave here for heaven, we will be "glorified." We might conjecture that since our Lord left His blood to minister to the earth, His veins are now filled with glory!

The blood is both a connector and a separator. It separates us from the clutches of the enemy and cleanses us so that we can be connected to the Lord. The blood cleanses, the oil heals, and the glory follows!

Another factor that connects us with the Lord and with each other is trust. The more we trust Him and others, the closer our relationships will be, on both the spiritual and the natural levels. Honor and commitment are equal parts of this dynamic. We certainly cannot be comfortably connected to someone we do not trust.

What an obedient heart it must have taken for Ananias to go at God's command to minister to Paul, the church's sworn enemy! We see that the Lord was working on both sides, in Paul and Ananias, with visions and instructions. In the end,

Paul received his sight back and was baptized. His miraculous transformation showed the believing community that Paul had truly changed.

The church, especially the Jerusalem church, doubted Paul's conversion for some years—so much so that they sent him home to Tarsus for several years until things cooled down. When the church needed Paul, kind-hearted Barnabas went to bring him back to Antioch where Paul was then able to step into his leadership calling.

We respond to the Lord and to people from our human spirit, even before we are born again and reconnected with God. Faith is one of the ways we respond to Him. He pours out His grace, and faith responds with a resounding *yes!* Believing His Word is a major connection point.

Numerous scriptures validate our Lord's desire that we be one with Him and each other. *For both He who sanctifies and those who are being sanctified are all of one, for which reason He is not ashamed to call them brethren, saying: "I will declare Your name to My brethren; in the midst of the assembly I will sing praise to You." And again: "I will put My trust in Him." And again: "Here am I and the children whom God has given Me"* (Heb. 2:11–13).

The prayer of faith is also a mighty connector. It connects us to Jesus and each other by the glory. We enter into another spiritual realm when we pray believing prayers. Paul acknowledged the way believers connected together in praying for one another. He said in 2 Corinthians 9:14, *And by their prayer for you, who long for you because of the exceeding grace of God in you.*

Of course, the primary connection we have in the Spirit is love. This is the proof of the pudding, so to speak, that we love one another. In his first epistle, the apostle John, who had an amazing revelation of the love of God, wrote, *If we say we have an intimate connection with the Father but we continue stumbling around in darkness, then we are lying because we do not live according to truth. If we walk step by step in the light, where the Father is, then we are ultimately connected to each other through the sacrifice of Jesus, His Son. His blood purifies us from all our sins"* (1 John 1:6–7 The Voice). These verses affirm a word I received from the Lord in February 2014: *"The blood heals the disconnect, and the glory glues it back."*

In his classic speech to the Puritans, John Winthrop said,

The definition which the Scripture gives us of love is this: Love is the bond of perfection [see Col. 3:14]. First, it is a bond or ligament. Secondly, it makes the work perfect. There is no body but consists of parts and that which knits these parts together, gives the body its perfection, because it makes each part so contiguous to others as thereby they do mutually participate with each other, both in strength and infirmity, in pleasure and pain. To instance in the most perfect of all bodies: Christ and His Church make one body. The several parts of this body considered a part before they were united, but when Christ comes, and by His spirit and love knits all these parts to himself and each to other, it is become the most perfect and best proportioned body in the world (Eph. 4:15–16). Christ, by whom all the body being knit together by every joint for the furniture thereof, according to the effectual power which is in the measure of every perfection of parts, a glorious body, without spot or wrinkle; the ligaments hereof being Christ, or His love, for Christ is love (1 John 4:8). So this definition is right. Love is the bond of perfection.[1] Near the end of the speech, Winthrop instructs them to

. . . follow the counsel of Micah, to do justly, to love mercy, to walk humbly with our God [see Mic. 6:8]. For this end, we must be knit together, in this work, as one man. We must entertain each other in brotherly affection. We must be willing to abridge ourselves of our superfluities, for the supply of others' necessities. We must uphold a familiar commerce together in all meekness, gentleness, patience and liberality. We must delight in each other; make others' conditions our own; rejoice together, mourn together, labor and suffer together, always having before our eyes our commission and community in the work, as members of the same body. So shall we keep the unity of the spirit in the bond of peace. The Lord will be our God, and delight to dwell among us, as His own people, and will command a blessing upon us in all our ways, so that we shall see much more of His wisdom, power, goodness and truth, than formerly we have been acquainted with.[2]

The same principles Winthrop speaks of apply to us, no matter what time frame our assignment on earth includes. As Arthur Burk, one of my favorite Bible teachers, frequently says, "Noble subjects keep doing what is right."[3]

Paul likewise pleaded with the church in Corinth in his first letter, *My brothers and sisters, I urge you by the name of our Lord Jesus, the Anointed, to come together in agreement. Do not allow anything or anyone to create division among you. Instead, be restored, completely fastened together with one mind and shared judgment* (1 Cor. 1:10 The Voice).

The beloved apostle John confirmed this thought, saying, *What we saw and heard we pass on to you so that you, too, will be connected with us intimately and become family. Our family is united by our connection with the Father and His Son Jesus, the Anointed One; and we write all this because retelling this story fulfills our joy* (1 John 1:3–4 The Voice).

The relationship of the Trinity is our primary example of connection. The honor the Father, Son, and Spirit give each other in the Word is the best picture we have of a healthy, life-giving relationship.

The Father spoke highly of His Son, saying, *"This is My beloved Son, in whom I am well pleased. Hear Him!"* (Matt. 17:5). The Word reports this incident seven times.

The Son also highly magnified the Father, saying, *"When you lift up the Son of Man, then you will know that I am He, and that I do nothing of Myself; but as My Father taught Me, I speak these things. And He who sent Me is with Me. The Father has not left Me alone, for I always do those things that please Him* (John 8:28–29).

Jesus said many honoring things about the Holy Spirit to come, as well.

Our connection with the Lord that makes it possible to be connected to each other in the Spirit. Paul writes, *Holding fast to the Head, from whom all the body, nourished and knit together by joints and ligaments, grows with the increase that is from God* (Col. 2:19).

Connecting the Dots

As we go through our days, we often think that incidents and circumstances just "happen." Some are pleasant and some are not. It is amazing that most people do not recognize the connections between many of these incidents.

It is good to realize that the Lord desires a great deal of involvement in our daily lives. He has the capacity to orchestrate events and work them to our advantage. If we are alert, we will see His Hand helping us through many incidents. *The key is joyous connection with Him and giving Him the glory!*

I watched Him work throughout my recent interstate move to provide the perfect timing for the sale of my long-time residence, help me sort out and give away many belongings, and then supply, quite last-minute, a residence in my new location.

A few days ago, I walked out to my car to run a short errand. Because I had workers doing a project in my driveway, I'd parked in a nearby spot and had to approach my car from the rear. Just as I got into the driver's seat, the workers returned from their lunch break. One of them jumped out his vehicle and ran over to my car. He said, "Don't start your car! You have a flat on the front tire!" Then he offered to change the tire, and did so. I was on my way in a few minutes and added a trip to the tire-repair shop to my to-do list. Long story short, I was saved a ruined tire, and the timing had to be the Lord!

The great part about these incidents is that I can now talk about them to perfect strangers and testify how the Lord helped me. He wants His presence to be a witness to the world through us!

I believe all of us can look back over our lives and distinctly see how our Lord has had a hand in working out circumstances in our behalf. Opportunities that were extraordinary, unexpected blessings, changes of direction—at the time we may not have seen how significant they were, but from our vantage point now, we can see it was clearly His doing.

Some events may have occurred that seemed like a disaster at the time, and we may've had to go to new levels of dependence on Him. Now, twenty or thirty years later, we can see how He still worked it for our good by the upward move it caused in our lives. Our worldview broadened, our compassion for others increased, and other good growth took place in our hearts, even in hard situations.

When our lives are as random as a Rubik's cube, He can still bring them into order. This truth gives new clarity to the beloved verse in Romans 8:28, *And we know that God causes everything to work together for the good of those who love God and are called according to his purpose for them* (NLT).

Once we realize that God is truly working things together for good in our lives, we will be more attentive each day. We will honor Him as soon as something happens because we will have seen His hand at work with our spiritual eyes. Then we will give a fresh witness—soon and often!

Communication

Communication is the key to healthy connections. It is life giving in both touch and words! Father has given us His Word to live by. Think how it has had to be protected and passed along through the ages. His message to us emphasizes that our communication with each other is especially vital.

"If My people who are called by My name will humble themselves, and pray and seek My face, and turn from their wicked ways, then I will hear from heaven, and will forgive their sin and heal their land" (2 Chron. 7:14–15).

Much of the time, we don't even see our own wicked ways, much less turn from them. With regard to communication, a "wicked way" might be our having a critical spirit and missing what the other person is trying to say. We need to be aware that, oftentimes, the enemy twists words between the mouth of the speaker and the ear of the hearer. If we're the one who's supposed to be listening, we must ask ourselves if we're listening with the "ear of our heart" to really understand what the other person is sharing with us. More than likely, we're gathering arguments to refute what we *think* that person is about to say, which makes our connection go awry.

As Louis and I prayed for better communication after we came to the Lord, we saw how hard the enemy works to disrupt our connecting. For several years we were so poor at articulating our views that we "prayed them on" each other, asking the Lord to tell the other what we were trying to share. He did help us for a while. Then He said we had grown to the level we could share without getting "soulish."

Once we saw that the enemy was actually twisting our words to try to keep us from receiving them correctly, we began to bind the "spirit of *perceptra*" and the "fowls of the air" so that they could not interfere.

An enormous amount of communication goes on in our world today. Computers and mobile devices. Sales pitches. Entertainment. Manipulation. Self-interest-centered appeals. Alarming news. Not to mention the skewed interchanges between fallible humans: "You said this!" "No, I did not!" "I don't remember promising that!"

Long story short, everyone is doing his own thing. Perhaps our day is reminiscent of the era conveyed in the final verse of Judges: *In those days there was no king in Israel; everyone did what was right in his own eyes"* (21:25).

We must look honestly at our interactions. We stumble around trying to articulate the things we mean to share, yet we often have not clarified them to ourselves. We repeatedly excuse our inept way of saying what is in our heart—and then blame it all on the one we are trying to communicate with. Worse still, we expect our spouse or children to read our mind!

With our peers, our goal should be to allay hostility and have an atmosphere of clear understanding. The Ephesians 6 description of God's armor portrays *truth* as "a belt." Belts are held up by belt loops. If we are stuck on one viewpoint, we are like a belt loop: we only see one little portion of the belt. We should want to hear other views, from other perspectives, so that we begin to see the whole scope of the belt. None of us are wise enough to see the entire picture by ourselves. We need the Lord's wisdom. Then we can learn to accept correction or rebuke, humble ourselves, and see the situation from Father's perspective.

If we really care about our spouse and our friends, we will learn to listen to them with our heart. We will keep pressing until we understand the treasures they have in their hearts!

One way to listen to someone else's heart is to restate what the person said. Try responding with this: "If I hear your heart, you're saying _____." Stay with it until the person is satisfied you have truly heard him. This listening skill is a difficult but necessary part of communication. We have to listen as carefully to other people as we do to the Lord.

"Keeping our *heart*" is essential: we must ask the Holy Spirit to help us learn to "*hear*"t with the h"*ear*"t of our *heart*. The reward of doing so is that the person we "*hear*"t will want to work to "*hear*"t us clearly and deeply also. This technique is another way we can mine the treasure in each other. As 1 John 2:20 says, *But you have an anointing from the Holy One, and you know all things.*

It's not hard to see that children pattern their parents' interactions. As such, we must learn the skills of validating one another. We must work at listening and sharing so that we can communicate from our heart. Doing so is part of the work required for having successful marriages and families. Enjoy with them things that give them joy. When problems arise that we can't talk through and resolve, we should quickly seek objective, godly counsel that is unbiased and Word based. A challenging, difficult time is not the time to seek sympathy for our point of view.

We can easily overlook the power of agreement. My husband and I came into agreement in prayer for one of our children when we were mere babies in the Lord. We began to practice Romans 4:17: *God, who quickeneth the dead, and calleth those things which be not as though they were* (KJV). Louis had been very angry with our daughter for her distressing behaviors. We agreed to begin praying for her according to this scripture.

A friend helped Louis see that his anger was really unforgiveness. Louis repented and cleared his heart. We began to speak a positive faith statement over every area that was painful. Louis even made a list!

We did not yet know enough Scripture to have a verse for each area of pain. Father honored our efforts to speak well of our daughter in our prayers and daily communication. It was a great change from the blaming and hand-wringing we had been doing! Amazingly, our speech changed our hearts toward her, and it changed her life. She came to know the reality of Jesus. She prayed the "sinner's prayer" with us on the fortieth day after we'd begun to pray. We learned several things. Here are two: (1) parental agreement is a formidable weapon, and (2) a faith transaction in the Spirit realm has great authority and power.

A similar dynamic occurs in families is when parents, two or more children, or a parent and child come into a *negative* agreement about another family member. In essence, the negative agreement curses that other family member, which keeps him from breaking free from the enemy's trap.

Thank God for the blood of Jesus! When we repent, the blood severs and melts away all negative agreements we've made with our words. In ministering to people over the years, we have seen firsthand the wonderful effect repentance and cleansing by the blood bring. We have also seen the reverse.

One time a couple asked us to share our testimony regarding the victory our daughter experienced after we repented and came into agreement for on her behalf (see story above). But these parents refused to accept the promise of, or responsibility for, what could happen if they changed the way they were speaking about and dealing with their child.

Neither did they experience the victory we'd had. Oh, what Father can do if we will give Him our words to work with!

We can train ourselves to make sure that what comes out of our mouths is honorable, true, and a blessing. Our words are immensely powerful. After all, our Father created the world with His words, and since we're created to be like Him, we have the ability to create with our words as well. Most of us shrink from the responsibility of guarding our words, but the fact that they hold creative power is an amazing truth. If we will embrace and honor this responsibility, it will bring blessing and order, not only to our lives, but to other people's lives as well.

I recall an incident that happened when I was very young in the Lord. (Oh, how He has helped me grow since then!) I was an expediter at my work: I specified and ordered the materials we needed for our large projects. A particular factory manufactured many of those materials according to the drawings we sent them. One day we received some items this supplier had constructed improperly. The materials did not match our drawings. As I was making the "usual speech" about the ineptness of the factory, all of a sudden, it seemed to me the words coming from my mouth were like small snakes and toads. The image was *so* yucky that I quickly "got the picture" the Lord was giving me, and from that day on, never made such a speech again. Of course, through the years I've had to be careful not to bite off the end of my tongue as I stopped short when I was tempted to say something I shouldn't.

We form all of our connections by interactions at multiple levels. Some are vertical. For instance, we look up to God and our parents and learn about authority and how it works. Unless we honor those in authority over us, we cannot receive the blessings God intended to flow down to us. Likewise, we will not properly exercise authority on behalf of those under us unless we are allowing this downward flow.

We find a lovely illustration of this principle in Psalm 133: *Behold, how good and how pleasant it is for brethren to dwell together in unity! It is like the precious oil upon the head, running down on the beard, the beard of Aaron, running down on the edge of his garments. It is like the dew of Hermon, descending upon the mountains of Zion; for there the LORD commanded the blessing—life forevermore.* Mount Hermon is the watershed of northern Israel. The mountains around Jerusalem, Mount Zion, are very dry. The water must flow south if the land is to be watered.

Again, if we let blessing flow down to us by honoring authority, our Lord, and our parents, we will then be able to let this blessing flow downward. Several spiritual principles function this way, including the anointing. We have only as much anointing as we receive from the Lord. If His Spirit is not pouring out into us, we have nothing to pour out into those under our authority.

Of course, we have many diverse communications on the horizontal level. Those relationship communications help us know who we are. Through other people's feedback, we see ourselves as they see us. The way we respond to them identifies our values and viewpoints. Working to get our ideas across helps us clarify our own thoughts. We can be an immense blessing to others as we use words wisely. God designed us to communicate this way.

In the following diagram of concentric circles, we can locate ourselves to see how well we have yielded our communication to the Lord in each area. If we are not honest with ourselves here, we won't be able to be honest in larger areas. The more we use our words to bless people closest to us, the more likely we'll use our words to bless those in our outer spheres of influence.

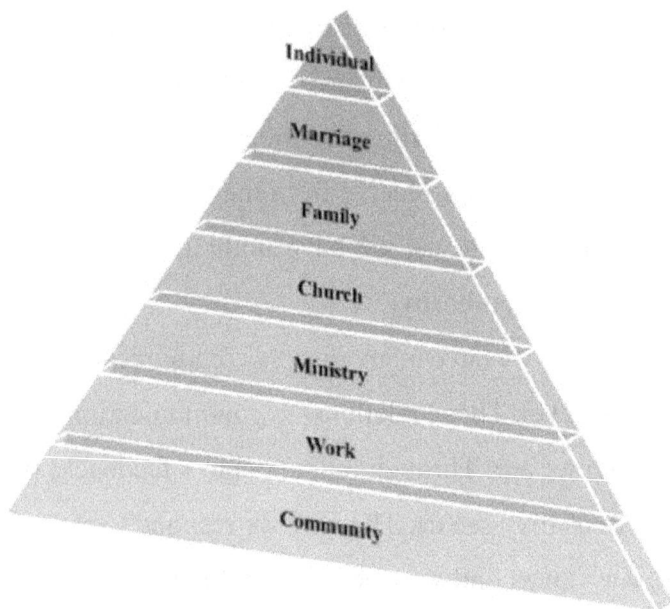

As we grow and mature in the Lord, so we should grow in exercising dominion over our "old man," the "old nature" we walked in before we received Christ. Once we have gained victory over our own life—what some refer to as "self-government"—we should then expand our influence to the next level: our marriage. Once our marriage is brought under the lordship of Christ, we should expand to our nuclear family, or household, and then to our property, neighborhood, church, community, city, state, and nation.

This model of expansion is God's design for bringing His kingdom (rule, dominion) to bear in the earth. As such, we can think of the above diagram as "concentric circles of dominion."

We see this same pattern of expansion in the political realm. We don't just wake up one day and say, "I want to be president of the United States!" No, first we run for the school board or the local town council. Once we have gained experience at that level, we run for mayor or for a seat on the county commission. Then it is on to a state-level job and next to governor. Once we have become a proven leader at that level, we can then aspire to a higher office, and so on.

As long as we are on the earth, there will always be work to do. God created us for work, for dominion, for ever-increasing levels of positive influence—for His glory, His name, and His kingdom! The trouble is, most believers see *work* as a four-letter word! They would rather just "rapture out of here" instead of taking responsibility for how the earth is being managed on their watch.

A child always wants to get what he wants, when he wants it. But an authority figure who really loves the child will not be so permissive. A responsible authority figure will lovingly train the child to wait for the appropriate time to receive the item or to work hard to earn it; or perhaps the person in authority will show the child why getting the item would not be good for him.

Scripture assures us that a father who loves his son will discipline that son. This pattern is especially true when it comes to communication. We copy the verbal patterns of our parents and other authority figures. For example, a father's voice may be loud or soft, but it will certainly be reflected in the way his children speak to him and each other. As such, parents, teachers, and other authority figures have an obligation to set a worthy example.

We should also have a goal of being totally honest—with ourselves and others. Total honesty describes our Father's character. Jesus Himself said, *"If you abide in My word, you are My disciples indeed. And you shall know the truth, and the truth shall make you free"* (John 8:31–32). Jesus used the words *"I tell you the truth"* eighty times in the gospels and even told Pilate that the reason He was born was to testify to the truth (see John 18:37).

If the truth sets us free, what does deception do? It binds us up, of course. That's another reason why total honesty should always be one of our goals.

People who have not been taught good communication skills may feel as though they shouldn't talk about their opinions if they're too challenging to others who don't share the same opinion. But having a differing opinion is not wrong. While it's not necessary to be harsh or belligerent when sharing an opinion, it's all right to have a unique way of looking at something. In fact, the more viewpoints that are presented, the better, more complete picture we may have.

We do have confrontations to meet in life, and not just with other people. Often we are required to confront our own desires and assumptions. Loving communication helps us become comfortable with who we are and why we think as we do. We should always remain teachable, because we really don't know "everything."

Our heavenly Father is a communicator. He created us as "speaking spirits." He designed us for communication with

Him and each other. Early in the Word, we see the importance of speaking. After the flood, the Lord blessed Noah and his sons: *"And as for you, be fruitful and multiply; bring forth abundantly in the earth and multiply in it." Now the sons of Noah who went out of the ark were Shem, Ham, and Japheth. And Ham was the father of Canaan. These three were the sons of Noah, and from these the whole earth was populated"* (Gen. 9:7, 18–19). Shem followed the Lord and was the ancestor of Abraham. The other two sons followed the way of the flesh and not God.

In Genesis 11:1–9, we find the following account:

Now the whole earth had one language and one speech. And it came to pass, as they journeyed from the east, that they found a plain in the land of Shinar, and they dwelt there. Then they said to one another, "Come, let us make bricks and bake them thoroughly." They had brick for stone, and they had asphalt for mortar. And they said, "Come, let us build ourselves a city, and a tower whose top is in the heavens; let us make a name for ourselves, lest we be scattered abroad over the face of the whole earth."

But the LORD came down to see the city and the tower which the sons of men had built. And the LORD said, "Indeed the people are one and they all have one language, and this is what they begin to do; now nothing that they propose to do will be withheld from them. Come, let Us go down and there confuse their language, that they may not understand one another's speech." So the LORD scattered them abroad from there over the face of all the earth, and they ceased building the city. Therefore its name is called Babel, because there the LORD confused the language of all the earth; and from there the LORD scattered them abroad over the face of all the earth."

The Lord had originally told the people to scatter, but they'd been determined to stay together. After the fall of the Tower of Babel, they were scattered because of the language barrier. Later, after coming out of Egypt, God told them they would be scattered from their new homeland if they were disobedient (see Deut. 4 and other references). Still, He gave them many promises that He would gather them back to the land and Himself.

We want to understand God's heart! He is the model for all communication.

Good communication in our relationships requires kindness, love, commitment, honesty, and openness. Healthy communication always involves a measure of transparency to work through the issues of life. It's all right for each of us to be our unique self, for the Lord designed it that way. Being different is not difficult when we are committed to the Lord. We each determine how we are going to live out His ways and assignments. We each take responsibility for following His guidelines for life, whether at home, at work, or elsewhere.

A fundamental reason to have good communication skills is to help those whose lives intertwine with ours. Our standard and foundation is the Word of God. We can communicate clearly to our children God has set universal, spiritual laws in place. It's up to us to demonstrate that His laws work for our benefit and blessing, and that they build a foundation for our lives.

If we base our lives on solely on our own interests, we will have a difficult time—our foundation will be weak. (If we walk on sand, we'll quickly discover it shifts daily.)

That's why it is key that we communicate truth to our loved ones and help them learn to trust our heavenly Father.

Sometimes when we face severe challenges, having a strong foundation is the only thing that will bring us through. In the Old Testament story of Joseph, we find a prime example of someone whose solid foundation carried him through (see Gen. 37, 39–48). The preference Joseph's father, Jacob, gave Joseph showed him that he had a special destiny. His dreams from God gave him hope when his life took a terrible turn, and he was faithful to the foundation his father had instilled in him, a foundation of trusting in God. As such, Joseph was eventually the one who saved his entire family—a family from whose lineage our Lord Jesus also came.

As God's children, we have a destiny and purpose. This truth is one of the main factors we are to communicate to the generations that follow us. Through every word we speak and every deed we do, we must convey to them that God has designed them (and every other person) for a special reason—and that life's greatest adventure is to discover this reason.

The Lord gives us clear instructions in Ephesians 4:25–5:10:

Therefore, putting away lying, "Let each one of you speak truth with his neighbor," for we are members of one another. "Be angry, and do not sin": do not let the sun go down on your wrath, nor give place to the devil. Let him who stole steal no longer, but rather let him labor, working with his hands what is good, that he may have something to give him who has need. Let no corrupt word proceed out of your mouth, but what is good for necessary edification, that it may impart grace to the hearers. And do not grieve the Holy Spirit of God, by whom you were sealed for the day of redemption. Let all bitterness, wrath, anger, clamor, and evil speaking be put away from you, with all malice. And be kind to one another, tenderhearted, forgiving one another, even as God in Christ forgave you.

Therefore be imitators of God as dear children. And walk in love, as Christ also has loved us and given Himself for us, an offering and a sacrifice to God for a sweet-smelling aroma.

But fornication and all uncleanness or covetousness, let it not even be named among you, as is fitting for saints; neither filthiness, nor foolish talking, nor coarse jesting, which are not fitting, but rather giving of thanks. For this you know, that no fornicator, unclean person, nor covetous man, who is an idolater, has any inheritance in the kingdom of Christ and God. Let no one deceive you with empty words, for because of these things the wrath of God comes upon the sons of disobedience. Therefore do not be partakers with them.

For you were once darkness, but now you are light in the Lord. Walk as children of light (for the fruit of the Spirit is in all goodness, righteousness, and truth), finding out what is acceptable to the Lord.

We want to be sure our words agree with Father's heart. He has left nothing to guesswork. He loves us and wants us to love each other! The Holy Spirit, the Helper, the *Paraclete*, who comes alongside to help us, desires to communicate with you! Connect with Jesus as Word! He has not spoken in secret! He has let us in on the secrets of a life well lived!

For thus says the LORD,

Who created the heavens,

Who is God,

Who formed the earth and made it,

Who has established it,

Who did not create it in vain,

Who formed it to be inhabited:

"I am the LORD, and there is no other.

I have not spoken in secret,

In a dark place of the earth;

I did not say to the seed of Jacob,

'Seek Me in vain';

I, the LORD, speak righteousness,

I declare things that are right."

—Isaiah 45:18–19

Notes

CHAPTER ONE

1. Deborah Raney, "Weaving It All Together," Write Well, Sell Well Conference (Crossings Community Center; Oklahoma City, OK), September 21, 2013.
2. Randy Alcorn, *Dominion* (New York: Multnomah Books, 1996), 498–502.
3. James Strong, *Strong's Exhaustive Concordance of the Bible* (Grand Rapids: Baker Book House, 1978), s.v. "sacrifice."

CHAPTER THREE

1. Dr. Bill Gillham, *Lifetime Guarantee* (Eugene: Harvest House Publishers, 1993), 114.
2. Carol Gordon, *Marriage Is a Gift* (Bethany: Heart Menders Publishing, 2007), 42–43.
3. Ibid.
4. Strong, s.v. "Abaddon"; "Apollyon."

CHAPTER FOUR

1. Ibid., s.v. "husband."
2. Ibid., s.v. "frame."

CHAPTER FIVE

1. Dr. Caroline Leaf, conversation with Kenneth and Gloria Copeland, *Believer's Voice of Victory*, Daystar and TBN, June 22, 2016. (In addition, Dr. Leaf noted that "quantum physics is all about relationships and connections.")
2. Strong, s.v. "touch."

3. Cheri Fuller, "Tell Me a Story: The Reality of Oklahoma's Children of Incarcerated Parents," OKDHS Practice and Policy Lecture Series (Oklahoma History Center; Oklahoma City, OK), February 17, 2012.

4. Dr. Paul Brand and Philip Yancey, *Pain: The Gift Nobody Wants* (Grand Rapids: HarperCollins Publishers and Zondervan Publishing House, 1993).

CHAPTER SEVEN

1. John Winthrop, *A Model of Christian Charity,* www.winthropsociety.com/doc_charity.php (accessed 6/15/16)

2. Ibid

3. Arthur Burk, www.theslg.com (accessed 7/12/16)

Recommended Reading

By CAROL GORGON

TOOLS FOR RULING AND REIGNING

By CAROL GORGON

MARRIAGE IS A GIFT

By CAROL GORGON

THE CHILD HEART
(also available in Spanish)

Leader and Study Guides are available with each book.

We also have a booklet for beginners in the Christian life called **"Body Basics, Spiritual Fitness for the Believer"**. It is an excellent for handout to new converts or for Sunday school classes.

These books are available from AMAZON for copy or digital download for your convenience.

Mailing Address:
PO BOX 141
Eastland, Texas 76448-0141
Email Address:
carolgordon@heartmenders.org
Best Contact Number:
(254) 488-2645

Visit our Websites

HeartMenders.org

HealingYourLand.org

Social Media Sites

YouTube.com/HeartMendersInc

Facebook.com/HeartMendersIntl

Facebook.com/HealingYourLand

Trending Topics On-Line

#HeartMenders
#HeartMendersIntl
#HealingYourLand
#TheChildHeart

Heart Menders International is 100% dedicated to a teaching, prayer and healing ministry. Regular meetings in the home, over the phone and online is how we communicate and celebrate the Word. We are available to minister at other churches as the Lord leads.

All of the teaching material from Heart Menders Healing seminars are now available on our website to view online at:

www.HealingYourLand.org

www.ingramcontent.com/pod-product-compliance
Lightning Source LLC
Chambersburg PA
CBHW052111090426
42741CB00009B/1766